MY AN(
WERE IN THE
SALVATION ARMY

HOW CAN I FIND OUT MORE ABOUT THEM?

Ray Wiggins

Society of Genealogists

Published by

Society of Genealogists
14 Charterhouse Buildings
Goswell Road
London EC1M 7BA

Registered Charity No. 233701

First edition 1997
Second edition 1999

Second edition © Society of Genealogists 1999

ISBN 1 85951 406 5

British Library Cataloguing in Publication Data

A CIP Catalogue record for this book is available from the British Library

CONTENTS

ILLUSTRATIONS

ACKNOWLEDGEMENTS

The author would like to express his gratitude to the numerous people who have given their time and effort in providing advice and information which has been invaluable in the production of this book. Included among these are the staff of Salvation Army archives and other departments in the United Kingdom, Australia, Canada, New Zealand and the United States of America.

Particular thanks are given to Jean Tooke of the Society of Genealogists for her comments and suggestions on the original draft and to Gordon Taylor of the Salvation Army International Heritage Centre for his direction to additional sources and, particularly, for checking the accuracy of the final draft.

Finally, to The Salvation Army for granting permission to reproduce the illustrations used.

INTRODUCTION

The Salvation Army is an organisation known throughout the world but the very name conjures up different thoughts in different people's minds. Those who have seen active service in wars or as civilians in the Blitz remember Red Shield mobile canteens turning up in the most remote places to provide much welcome tea and refreshments. Some think of the social and goodwill work carried out by Salvationists while other thoughts are of brass bands or of searching for missing persons.

Nevertheless, it must be stressed that the Army has from its inception been first and foremost a denomination of the Christian Church. Indeed its Articles of Faith, or doctrines, are based on the holy scriptures and the early Christian creeds. This fact was recognised as long ago as 1880 when the then Editor of *The Independent Methodist Magazine*, a Mr Brunlow, speaking at a meeting in Bolton, said: 'There are three things in which I cannot see much difference, a column of The War Cry, a page of Wesley's Journal and a chapter of the Acts of the Apostles'.

Other books in this series have listed what registers exist and where they may be found. As to records of The Salvation Army, there is a vast amount of material available but, as far as birth, marriage and death registers are concerned, the family historian will find few, if any, have survived. However, this is not such a problem as with other churches because the Army came into being many years after civil registration was introduced into this country.

Remembering that family history is closely allied to local and social history, it is hoped that this publication will enlighten those readers whose ancestors were either Salvationists themselves or closely associated with the Army as to something of its background, what further information may be available and some of the unusual terminology used.

WILLIAM AND CATHERINE BOOTH

To talk about the Salvation Army one must start with William Booth. A man years ahead of his time; a great preacher, a great social reformer and a great businessman. He is still affectionately referred to by Salvationists as the 'Founder' but this term is a misnomer as the development of the Army was more an evolution than the efforts of one man setting out to found a new branch of the Christian Church. In fact, like Billy Graham today, he hoped initially that his converts would link up with one of the established churches, but this was not to be.

He was born in Nottingham in 1829, the son of Samuel Booth and his wife, Mary Moss, and baptised into the Anglican Church at Sneinton. It has been suggested that Mary was a Jewess, but this fact has never been established and is most unlikely, despite the fact that her features certainly had a strong Jewish resemblance. Samuel was an unsuccessful speculative builder and died when William was fourteen years old and at the time working as a pawnbroker's apprentice. Being the eldest surviving son, he had to support his widowed mother and two younger sisters. At the age of seventeen he received his first appointment as a local preacher and from then on he had a varied preaching career before, to quote his own words, he 'found his destiny'.

Having completed his apprenticeship, and now unemployed, he moved to London to seek work and lodgings. There he continued as a lay preacher with the Wesleyan Methodists but, as there was not enough pulpit work for him, he started open-air work on his own in Kennington. He then joined the Methodist Reform Movement, preaching at Binfield Road Chapel, Clapham, where his future wife and her mother were members of the congregation.

At one stage during this period he even considered becoming a Congregational minister, but after careful consideration, felt that he could not accept the Calvinistic basis of Congregational theology. So, for eighteen months, he took charge of the Reformers' Spalding Circuit. Back in London in 1854 he joined the Methodist New Connexion and conducted revival campaigns in many parts of the country. The following year the New Connexion Conference resolved that the Reverend William Booth should be appointed to the work of an evangelist.

In 1855 William married Catherine Mumford, born in Ashbourne, Derbyshire, the daughter of a Methodist lay preacher. She herself played a very active part in the development and administration of the Army, being a gifted preacher who addressed large public meetings throughout Britain with far-reaching results. She was certainly a pioneer of female ministry and one of the most remarkable women of the nineteenth century.

Many years ago one writer said prophetically of the Booths: 'When some future historian takes up his pen to describe the social progress of England during the latter half of the nineteenth century, there will be one family, neither rich, titled, nor politically conspicuous, whose work and influence it will be impossible to ignore.'

After their marriage William worked as a circuit minister in Halifax, Brighouse and Gateshead but felt that his calling was really as an evangelist, and dissatisfied with the limitations enforced upon him by the Conference, he decided, with the full support of his wife, to resign. From that time forward the conducting of missions in such places as Cornwall, Cardiff, Walsall and, finally, Leeds, became the life work of this devoted couple.

In 1865 they returned to London, first setting up home in Hammersmith; later the same year another move took them to the Hackney area. Here they lived for the next fifteen years, bringing up and educating their children while they themselves, unsparingly and enthusiastically continued their joint ministry.

Catherine's health had always been indifferent and at fifty- nine years of age she was diagnosed as suffering from cancer. William's distress at this news must have been devastating. He even put a request in *The War Cry* for anyone who knew of any cures for this disease to write to him personally. He eventually arranged for his wife to go to Clacton-on-Sea, in Essex, to rest. On the 4 October 1890 she died. Her body was brought back to London where it lay in state before being buried in Abney Park Cemetery, Stoke Newington, in a section where, later, other members of the family and many prominent officers were to be buried. For the funeral her son, Herbert, composed a tune, 'Promoted to Glory', which was to become the Army's funeral march.

Writing in *The War Cry* at the time William himself said: 'She was the *Army Mother*. Other religious organisations cannot be said to have a Mother; their guides and authorities are all *Fathers*. The Salvation Army has, of God's great mercy and wisdom, and we think through His own leading and inspiration, felt its need of the more tender, feminine side of human character, as well as the more robust and masculine element.' Catherine is still today revered and known by Salvationists as the 'Army Mother'.

4

William survived his beloved wife by 22 years. In 1912 he had a second cataract operation which left him totally blind and his strength quickly failed. On the 20 August of that year it was announced that General Booth had 'laid down his sword'. Tributes and messages of sympathy poured in from all over the world - from kings and queens, heads of state and other dignitaries, as well as ordinary people.

His funeral was as impressive as had been Catherine's before him. As his body lay in state in the Salvation Army Congress Hall, Clapton, 65,000 people came to pay homage to this great man and 35,000 attended the memorial service at Olympia, among them Queen Alexandra. When the cortège, with 7000 Salvationists and 40 bands processed from Victoria Embankment to Abney Park, the heart of London stood still for nearly four hours. As it passed the Mansion House the Lord Mayor stood to salute the coffin.

EARLY HISTORY

One evening in June 1865 William Booth found himself in the East End of London. Seeing besotted, poverty-stricken people crowding into the beer shops and gin palaces, his heart went out to them. As he approached the 'Blind Beggar' public house in Whitechapel Road - notorious in recent times as the place where Ronnie Kray shot George Cornell - a group of missioners were concluding an open-air meeting. The leader asked if any bystander would like to have a word and the Reverend William Booth accepted the invitation.

A few days later two members of the mission who had been impressed by his simple, forthright oratory, asked him if he would temporarily take charge of a tent mission on a disused burial ground. From that beginning the mission grew. After two months, however, the tent blew down and immediate arrangements were made to hold Sunday meetings in a dancing academy, still in existence in New Road, Whitechapel. From time to time all sorts of buildings were used; a skittle alley, a wool shed, a run-down public house and an adapted area under a railway arch. However, occasionally problems did arise. For example, in 1884 when a meeting was held in the 'Star and Garter Hotel' in Sheffield the congregation had to dispense with singing because the hotel was not licensed for vocal music.

Stations were opened in other places and, after changing its name two or three times, the mission became known as the Christian Mission with William Booth as its General Superintendent.

As the 1878 Annual Report and Appeal was being prepared a heading at the top of a page stated, 'The Christian Mission is a Volunteer Army'. William Booth's son, Bramwell, who was later to become his second-in-command and succeed him as General, objected to the word 'Volunteer'. Leaning over his shoulder, his father crossed it out, and wrote in the word 'Salvation'. By this time there were fifty stations throughout England and Wales manned by eighty-eight evangelists.

Almost by accident - some would say providential guidance - the organisation grew into an Army. One evangelist referred to the General Superintendant as the 'General' and called himself 'Captain'. Some people designed uniforms for themselves. Military terms were used, orders and regulations drafted, and the stations became known as corps. Where there was more than one corps in a town or city they would be distinguished by adding a number such as Leeds 1, Leeds 2, etc. Later, numbers were replaced by adding the name of the district in which they were situated; Liverpool Walton, Liverpool Old Swan, etc. Other names added would be Castle, Congress Hall and, the most common, Citadel. So the Army developed and grew.

But things were not always easy. Opposition, both verbal and physical, was met on all sides. More than one Salvationist died from wounds received at the hands of the mobs. Many times the police refused to protect them and magistrates would not convict those who attacked them. There was little sympathy from the press, either.

A typical vitriolic letter appeared in the *Willesden Chronicle*. the local paper of a London suburb. Among other things, the writer said: 'They parade the streets in front of other people's houses, singing (?), playing (?), shouting (?) ... a lot of densely ignorant ragamuffins ... annoying people who object to their impertinence ... a lot of greasy looking louts ... making hideous noises and boasting that they have led disreputable lives.'

During 1882 alone, it was reported that many soldiers and officers had been knocked down, kicked or otherwise brutally assaulted, 251 of them being women and 23 children under fifteen. Also, 56 of the buildings used by the Army had been seriously damaged.

Salvationists themselves were also prosecuted, convicted, fined and even sent to prison, often under local bye-laws, for such offences as obstructing the highway, preaching, praying, singing and playing musical intruments in the streets.

The matter came to a head in 1882 when Captain William Beatty and two soldiers were arrested for holding a procession in Weston-super-Mare. They refused to be bound over to keep the peace and were sentenced to three months' imprisonment. Successfully appealing to the Queen's Bench Division of the High Court, Mr Justice Field delivered a lengthy judgment which decided, once and for all, whether Salvationists should be suppressed or protected. He and his colleague rejected the magistrates' implication that 'a man may be punished for acting lawfully because he knows that his so doing may induce another man to act unlawfully'. The principles laid down in *Beatty v. Gillbanks (1882)* are still quoted in public order cases today.

OVERSEAS DEVELOPMENT

There were no plans to extend the work to other parts of the world but when Amos Shirley, his wife, and daughter, who as a sixteen-year-old girl was a Lieutenant, emigrated to the USA from Coventry in 1879 they started meetings in Philadelphia. The next year an officer, George Scott Railton, with seven women Salvationists, was sent out to commence the work officially.

The same year two men, John Gore and Edward Saunders, who had emigrated to Australia, met in a mission meeting in Adelaide. Discovering that they had both been converted in the Christian Mission they decided to conduct an open-air meeting in the city. Soon after, they each wrote to William Booth asking him to send somebody out to start the Army in Australia. However, they could not wait for this to happen, and when a few months later Captain and Mrs Thomas Sutherland arrived to take charge they found 68 Salvationists waiting to greet them. John Gore retired as an Adjutant and Edward Saunders as a Lieutenant Colonel. Descendants of both these men are serving as officers or local officers today.

Similarly two young men, eighteen-year-old Jack Addie and Joe Ludgate, commenced the work in Canada in 1882. Later Jim Cathcart, who had earlier been involved with Jack in holding cottage prayer meetings, linked up with him again and became an officer, remaining so for the rest of his life.

Yet another year later William Booth received a request from France asking him to come and carry out in Paris what he had done in London. At that time Paris was not a particularly safe place, especially for preachers. Nevertheless, he responded by sending his twenty-two-year-old daughter, Catherine, to do what had been requested. She was accompanied by two other young girls, nineteen-year-old Florence Soper, the daughter of a Welsh doctor, who later married Catherine's brother Bramwell, and Adelaide Cox, eighteen years of age, who had left a sheltered vicarage to become a Salvationist. To the Army her father was the 'General' but to the French Catherine, or Kate as she came to be known, was 'La Maréchale'.

In complete contrast, the work in India - the first missionary country - was commenced by Frederick St George de Lautour Tucker, a man of aristocratic background whose Devonshire family could be traced back to the sixteenth century and included knights, esquires, admirals, generals and judges. While working as an assistant commissioner in Dharmsala in the Himalayas he read about the work of the Army in a religious paper and sent a donation. With the receipt was a copy of *The War Cry* and he immediately took leave and came to England to learn more about the work. When he told William Booth he wanted to join his movement he was told to go away and find out more about it. Within about four months he had resigned from the India Civil Service and thrown in his lot with the Army. After a short period of familiarisation Tucker and three other officers arrived in Bombay in September 1882 to start the work.

And so the Army moved on to countries large and small; to Sweden (1882), St Helena (1884), Argentina (1890), Zimbabwe (1891), Japan (1895) and many more places until today it operates in about 100 countries throughout the world. In 1991 it returned to Russia and in 1993 to the Ukraine. In both these countries the work is expanding rapidly.

It must be pointed out that although the work in many countries was pioneered by people not only from the United Kingdom but other places as well, officers may be given appointments in any part of the world. One may, therefore, sometimes need to make enquiries in overseas territories for information about his ancestors.

SOCIAL WORK

Ever concerned about the poor and under-privileged, if William Booth saw a need he had to take steps to meet or alleviate that need as quickly as possible. Crossing London Bridge one December night in 1887, he was shocked to see men sleeping under the arches. The next morning he asked Bramwell if he was aware that this was going on. Bramwell admitted that he did and his father ordered him to go and do something about it. Less than three months later the first food and shelter depot was opened in Limehouse. Others were established in Cardiff, Edinburgh, Glasgow and other parts of the country to be followed further afield in Europe, North America, Australia and South Africa.

When he discovered that match-makers working at home were underpaid and worse still, suffered necrosis of the jaw-bone (or 'phossy jaw' as it was often called) through the inhalation and ingestion of white phosphorous, he opened a match factory producing matches using non-poisonous red phosphorous. Over 100 people were employed and they were paid four pence a gross, as against the old rate of two and a half pence.

Even in the days of the Christian Mission an attempt had been made to establish Rescue Homes to help girls who had fallen into prostitution to get away from such a life but it did not materialise for some years. In 1881 a runaway girl came to a meeting in Whitechapel and was counselled late at night by a Mrs Elizabeth Cottrill. Discovering the girl was living in a brothel, Mrs Cottrill took her to her own home in Christian Street, made her a bed on some chairs in the kitchen, and the next day accompanied her back to her parents in Brighton.

She continued this service in her home for three years until a house in Hanbury Street, just over half a mile away, was acquired so that the work for such girls could continue on a permanent basis. The previous year the first official Rescue Home had been opened in Glasgow.

Provision of homes for the aged - Eventide Homes - began in Australia in 1901, and in 1910 the Women's Social Work of Great Britain and Ireland opened a community home for elderly women. A Darby and Joan home, accommodating twenty couples, was later opened at Southborough, Kent. The first of the Men's Social Work homes was opened at Camberwell in south-east London in 1926, principally for men who had worked on the staff of the Army's institutions.

Yet another project was the opening of Prison Gate Homes, starting in Australia and spreading to other countries. Salvationists, some of whom were themselves converted ex-prisoners, literally met released criminals at the prison gate and took them to a home where they were housed, fed and encouraged to lead an honest life. Often work was also found for them to do. The authorities allowed officers to hold meetings in prisons and interview and counsel the prisoners. Before the legislation changed, the Army had a number of approved homes and still has bail hostels. Many officers today serve as prison chaplains.

During the same month that his wife Catherine died in 1890, William Booth published a book entitled *In darkest England and the way out*. It outlined his proposals for social reform, some of which had already been started. The first edition was sold out on the day of publication and a year later the sales figures were over 200,000. By the end of 1891 it had been translated into French, German, Swedish, Dutch and Japanese. It was reprinted again in 1970.

What was referred to as the 'Cab-Horse Charter' was set up. He said 'Every cab-horse in London has three things - a shelter for the night, food for its stomach, and work allotted to it for which it can earn its corn. When he is down he is helped up, and while he lives he has food, shelter and work.' 'How many people in England,' he asked, 'lived worse than the London cab-horse?'

The proposals, many of which soon materialised, were divided into three sections: the City Colony, the Farm Colony and the Overseas Colony, all of which would establish self-helping communities.

The City Colony would gather up the poor and destitute, supply their immediate pressing necessities, find them shelter and temporary employment and inspire them with a hope for the future. Work for the unemployed was split into the Factory and the Household Salvage Brigade, referred to as Elevators. It included training and employing people in such basic skills as brush and basket making, tinsmithing, carpentry, tailoring, tambourine making and sign-writing, etc. It also involved the collection of rags, newspapers and other waste material.

Six months earlier experiments had been carried out by the opening of a Labour Bureau and it was proposed that in all large towns and cities a central registry, free of charge, should be established. By 1897, 81,831 unemployed had been registered at the Bureaux and 69,119 had found temporary or permanent employment. It was not until 1909 that Parliament passed a Bill providing for the institution of Labour Exchanges.

Realising that all men and women were not suitable for the schemes covered by the City Colony, it was proposed that such people could be trained in many branches of agriculture, and 800 acres of land, later increasing to 3200 acres, was purchased in Hadleigh, Essex. Dormitories, a kitchen and dining room together with a hospital with sixteen beds were built. Here crops were cultivated, there were cattle, sheep, pigs and poultry, market gardens, workshops and greenhouses as well as a brickworks. During the first twenty-one years 6870 men were admitted and, of these, 4297 found suitable employment.

In January 1903 the Army's first secular elementary school was opened for children of the colonists and the villagers at Hadleigh. With the endorsement of H.M. Inspectorate, Staff Captain Collins was appointed the Headmaster and 108 names were registered. Earlier than this schools had been established in Newfoundland to meet a need created, on the one hand, by the denominational system of education which was the rule in the Dominion, there being no schools outside those provided by the various religious bodies, and on the other hand by the growth of the Army in that part of the world. There are now schools, some for blind, deaf and other handicapped children, run by qualified Salvationist teachers in many parts of the world, particularly the missionary countries.

William Booth considered the lack of thrift and care in the country to be appalling and when in 1891 he was approached to take over the Charter of the Methodist and General Assurance Society Ltd., he accepted it, changing the name to the Salvation Army Assurance Society in 1904.

Today there are organised emergency teams which go out whenever and wherever a disaster or accident occurs, to give refreshment to those involved in rescue, fire-fighting and policing and, more important, to counsel victims of such incidents. Also, every night, soup runs are organised, going round the larger cities and giving sustenance to the homeless sleeping on the streets.

MEDICAL WORK

It was a natural progression from the Rescue Homes to the establishment of a home where girls could go to have their babies, rather than to the workhouse. A small house in Chelsea was taken over for this purpose but some were cases where hospital treatment was needed and a maternity hospital, Ivy House, Hackney, was opened. After their confinement the girls were able to be looked after at another house until they were able to face the world again.

Nearly a quarter of a century later, in 1913, the Mothers' Hospital in Clapton took the place of Ivy House. It was opened by Princess Louise, who had laid the foundation stone the year before, and consisted of six large semi-detached houses connected by corridors with four bungalow wards erected at the rear.

Later, it developed into a training hospital for both Salvationist and non-Salvationist nurses and also a centre for district nurses. By August 1948 the total number of births had reached 100,000 and 2,600 midwives had been trained. After the Second World War the hospital became part of the National Health Service and was closed in 1986.

The overseas medical work of the Army was pioneered by one Harry (Henry John) Andrews, who was brought up in an Army home after his mother died. At the age of fifteen he went to India with William's daughter Emma and her husband. Becoming an officer himself, and with no medical training, he started an amateur dispensary in a small bathroom in Nagercoil. Later, Bramwell Booth arranged for him to go to Illinois University to qualify as a doctor. At the end of the First World War, when trouble arose on the North-West Frontier, the military authorities requisitioned his services, giving him the rank of Temporary Captain. One night, after attending the wounded following a heavy raid, he himself was killed. For his bravery he was posthumously awarded the Victoria Cross. Today the Army provides over 8000 beds in over 80 hospitals and nursing homes throughout the world.

ADOPTIONS AND FOSTERING

Following on from the opening of maternity hospitals, homes for orphans or children who had been abused were established and a Children's Aid Department was set up to deal with affiliation cases, arrange for the adoption of certain children and to have responsibility concerning nurse-mothers.

Affiliation work was difficult; the putative father had to be found, admission of his responsibility had to be extracted from him and then he had to be persuaded to contribute regularly to the child's support. Usually the money was paid to the Department from where it was passed to the mother who then made her own arrangements with the nurse-mother.

Nurse-mothers were selected by the Department with great care, each being visited and her references thoroughly checked before a child was entrusted to her.

Sometimes it was not practicable for the single mother to keep the child, or she may have married a man who objected to having the child as part of his family. Occasionally the mother died. In such cases it was necessary for adoption or fostering to be arranged. Many of these arrangements made by the Department turned out to be happy ones.

An announcement in *The War Cry* of the 25 March 1895 said: 'Mrs Bramwell Booth will be glad to hear of any soldier or friend, in or near London, who will be willing to receive one of our Rescue babies, to care for a while. This is often of the greatest help to the mother in her struggle to once more gain the way of virtue and truth.'

Even before this the Army operated an adoption scheme. There is evidence as early as 1888 of a childless couple in Peckham who were able to adopt a ten-year-old girl, born after her mother had separated from her lawful husband and who, through the Army's influence, had decided to leave the child's father and return to Scotland to seek her husband and other children.

Initially it was legally possible for parents or private organisations to arrange for a child to be placed with adoptive parents but now it must be done through a government-approved adoption agency.

The Army was an adoption society until the 1933 Adoption Act. After that it continued as an adoption agency but the information on children accommodated through agencies varies from one society to another. Some will not even disclose to the agency the place to which a child has been sent.

For further information see the reference to Social Services in the Archives and Memorabilia section.

EMIGRATION

The third section of the Darkest England scheme, the Overseas Colony, was not carried into effect in the manner and the degree to which the author had hoped. It was to be tracts of land in South Africa, Canada, Western Australia and elsewhere where the Army would govern and create homes for prodigals and the destitute, reforming them and creating in them habits of industry and honesty.

However, sponsored emigration had started in 1882 through James Hooker, an Australian ironfounder who played the clarinet and became the Bandmaster at Adelaide Congress Hall. While in England, combining a holiday with a government mission to search for emigrants, he put an advertisement in *The War Cry* for 'Fifty Blood and Fire Lassies' who were cooks, housemaids, or in general service for a free passage to Australia. A considerable number arrived in Adelaide the following year and found situations at once.

William Booth laid down that emigration should be helpful to the individual, acceptable to the old land and advantageous to the new country. So it was that an Emigration Advice Bureau was put into operation so that the suitability of the individual and the situation could be decided upon. In 1901 the first batch who had been trained at Hadleigh Farm Colony left for Canada under the charge of an Army officer, the voyage being made instructive and profitable. In 1908 the Army chartered three ships with seven sailings to Canada.

Sometimes it was advisable for a mother to establish herself in one of the colonies before being joined by her children. It such cases the children would be looked after in one of the Army's homes. Other children, of all ages and classes and in different circumstances, were accommodated at the request of outside agencies. For example, a two-year-old girl was taken from a home in England to her father in Detroit while a five-year-old orphan was conveyed to her uncle in New Zealand.

Between 1916 and 1923 many women and children taken from almost hopeless situations, some war widows and orphans, were established with bright prospects in Canada, South Africa, Australia and New Zealand.

This work continued until the outbreak of the Second World War, enabling some 250,000 people to start a new life in one or other countries of the New World. In one year alone, 25,000 migrants went to Canada.

<table>
<tr><td colspan="2">

The Salvation Army
SAILING SHEET (No Work)

S.S. LETITIA ——— from LIVERPOOL. ———

to ST. JOHN. ——— on 29/3/30. ——— 192——

LOAN——————**Class**————
This Loan does not include fee. Full details of Loan are shown on the Advice Note.

</td><td>

Case Registered No.

I.E.O. L. 6495.

Overseas————

Special Marks

Families grant,

£24- 14-5d.

A   C   I

</td></tr>
</table>

PASSENGER				LONDON	
PASSENGER AUSTIN **MRS.** MARY. *Age* 32					
Names of persons accompanying and age of each				PROVINCIAL	
Robert. 9. John 8. Elsie. 5. Dorothy 4.			1	4	–
			DESTINATION		
Married or Single Married. **Town** Liverpool.			**Town** Sandwich.		
Nationality English. *Present Occupation* Housewife.					
Religion C of E. OCEAN TICKET No. D.62298.			**Province or State** Ontario.		

	DATE	£	s.	d.
Deposit Paid		30	0	0
Balance „				
Order No rail. B.1659. $ 55-90.		11	12	11
„ „ Food. B.1660. $ 15-15.		3	3	3
„ „ $				
Home Rail Incidentals covered.				
Letter of Credit No. $				
„ „ *Charge*				
Letter of Authority No. $				
„ „ *Charge*				
Expenses prior to Sailing				
Joint ⎰ INSURANCE	*Particulars of Luggage insured*			
Luggage ⎱ POLICY No.				
Unemt.				

Name and Address of Friends Overseas :— Mr Robert Austin,

410, Peter Street West.   Sandwich.   Ontario.

In all cases of Prepaids and Passages partly paid
the Sailing Sheet is stamped with the name of the Territory in which the business originated.

DATE OF PASSENGER'S ARRIVAL

REPORT OF TICKETS, ETC., ISSUED OVERSEAS   *Employer's Application No.*

Name of Employer sent to

Occupation ·

Full P.O. Address

			PORT OF LANDING			Ticket Nos.
CANADA	Route	AUSTRALIA	NEW ZEALAND	SOUTH AFRICA		
Halifax, N.S.	C.P.R.	Freemantle	Wellington	Durban		
St. John, N.B.		Adelaide	Auckland	Port Elizabeth		
Quebec, P.Q.		Sydney				
Montreal, P.Q.		Melbourne				
Portland	C.N.R.	Brisbane				

Railway Station   *No. Tickets Required*

	£	s.	d.		£	s.	d.
████ No.				*Total Cost of Railway Tickets* ...			
Paid by Passenger				*Amount Refunded to Passenger* ...			
	Total			*Total*			

Sailing Sheet of emigrant to Canada - 1930

ORGANISATION AND ADMINISTRATION

In the early days committees of men who were not necessarily members of the Christian Mission were formed to assist in the running of it. The Mission's honorary legal advisor, Mr Frederick Whittaker, of Grays Inn, announced in March 1867 that a committee of which he was to be the secretary, was being established to relieve William Booth of the heavy responsibility of the financial support needed. A number of influential people served on this committee until 1876, by which time the work had been so established that it no longer needed financial backing.

Three years after the formation of the first committee William Booth assembled the first conference of the Mission to consider the elaborate constitution which he had devised. This was composed of 34 members with himself as the General Superintendent, the Secretary, treasurers, evangelists in charge of districts, life members, and two lay delegates. Records of these meetings have been preserved.

Rules of the Christian Mission were drafted relating to such matters as Bible classes, local preachers, a children's mission, open-air meetings, baptism and marriage, and mission property. One rule stated that female preachers would be eligible for employment as preachers, class leaders and any office and that they could speak and vote at all official meetings - this was 48 years before women over 30 years of age were allowed to vote in parliamentary elections! Two women were later to be elected as Generals of this world-wide Army, William's own daughter, Evangeline (1934-39) and Australian born Eva Burrows (1986-93).

By 1877 it was decided that government by committees was too slow and roundabout when decisions were continually required upon important matters. William Booth addressed the conference in the January of that year and, without any dissenting voice, it was agreed that the conference should continue, not as a legislative assembly, but as a council of war.

Today, for administrative purposes, the organisation is divided into territories under the command of a territorial commander. These usually cover the whole of a country, or, in countries of large geographical area like India and the USA, a number of territories exist. Territories are divided into divisions and divisions into corps or centres.

For many years the social services and public relations work were covered by separate administrative areas but in 1996 reorganisation in the United Kingdom brought these two functions into the same area as corps under the overall management of the divisional commander. The total number of divisions being eighteen.

Lieutenant's Commission and Appointment - 1891

OFFICERS AND SOLDIERS

A Salvation Army officer is a full-time paid minister of the Gospel, trained and employed by the Army, who, as already mentioned, may be appointed to any position in the world. In the early days they often stayed in one place for only a few months, thus making it sometimes difficult for the family historian to locate them. For married couples the work is considered to be a joint ministry and, therefore, active officers may only marry other officers, the wife taking the same rank as the husband. This rule no longer applies to retired officers.

Up to 1995 a married lady officer would be referred to, for example, as Mrs Major Smith, or in the case of one who still remained active after her husband had died, Major Mrs Smith. Now, whether married or single, she is referred to as Major Mary Smith.

At one time officers' ranks were not entirely accurately in line with those of military officers. In order of precedence they were:

Lieutenant
Captain
Ensign
Adjutant
Commandant
Staff Captain
Major (a Major in charge of a corps was at one time called a Field Major and, because of the colour of his trimmings, he was sometimes colloquially referred to as a 'Green Major').
Brigadier
Lieutenant Colonel
Colonel
Lieutenant Commissioner
Commissioner
General

Today the ranks are more streamlined, being:

Lieutenant
Captain
Major
Lieutenant Colonel
Colonel
Commissioner
General

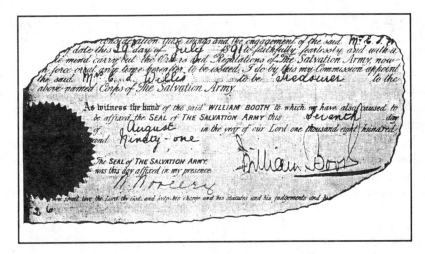

Treasurer's Certificate signed by William Booth - 1891

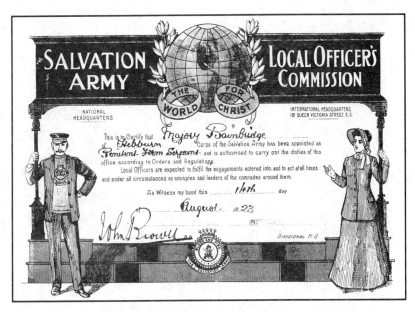

Local Officers Commission - 1923

There is only one General who is the head of the movement throughout the world. He is elected by a High Council of Commissioners and territorial commanders, who in the smaller territories, may have the rank of Colonel.

Although all Salvationists are soldiers of the Salvation Army - after St Paul's advice to the young Timothy to be 'a good soldier of Jesus Christ' - those who are not officers are distinguished by just being referred to by the generic term 'soldier'. These people may, however, have lay, unpaid positions and are referred to by titles such as Corps Secretary, Corps Sergeant Major, Bandmaster, Home League Secretary, etc. Such are known as local officers (see Glossary of Salvation Army Terms). Those with no specific position are referred to as Brother X or Sister Y. There is no rule that soldiers must only marry other Salvationists. All local officers and many soldiers, but not all, wear uniform. There have always been a number of full-time paid employees who are not officers and today many are not even Salvationists.

UNIFORMS

When the Christian Mission became an Army it was soon recognised that it would be fitting for a military type uniform to be adopted. Some men began wearing various types of helmets and caps adorned with home-made badges. Eventually, peaked caps with a red ribbon bearing the words 'The Salvation Army' and the Salvation Army crest became standard wear.

The crest was designed by Captain William H Ebdon and first appeared in 1879. Its emblems set forth the main doctrines of the Army: the round figure, the sun, represents the light and fire of the Holy Spirit; the cross is the cross of Jesus Christ; the 'S' stands for salvation; the swords stand for the swords of the warfare of salvation; the shots are the truth of the Gospel and the whole is surmounted by the crown of glory.

Mrs Booth noticed that women cadets who entered the first session at the Training Home for Officers in 1880 were wearing a variety of headgear. She therefore decided to design something that was large enough to protect the heads of the girls from the cold as well as from brickbats that might be thrown at them. With the help of her daughter, Emma, who at nineteen years of age had been appointed Principal of the Training Home, and Cadet Annie Lockwood, a milliner from Barnsley, the 'Hallelujah Bonnet' was produced. Some cadets objected to wearing such 'old-fashioned' bonnets but even today the Army bonnet, now much smaller but still based on the original design, is recognised everywhere.

It is popular today for people to wear tee-shirts with all sorts of logos or slogans printed on them. Over 100 years ago Salvationists wore guernseys with texts or 'Salvation Army' embroidered on them. The first official guernseys for men and women were blue, later changed to red, with either 'Salvation Army' or the Army crest on them.

These were followed by the wearing of tunics, officer's rank being distinguished by different coloured patches and trimmings on the collar with an insignia according to their rank, the epaulet being of the same colour with black braid edging it. All officers' patches are now coloured red. For a time headquarters officers wore the initials of the particular place where they worked on their epaulets, such as 'I.H.Q.' (International Headquarters), 'N.H.Q.' (National Headquaters) or 'S.A.A.S.' (Salvation Army Assurance Society).

In 1970 a lapel-style uniform was introduced in the United Kingdom with ladies having the choice of either still wearing the traditional bonnet or a bowler-style hat with, instead of the Salvation Army crest, a simple logo of a red shield bearing the words 'The Salvation Army'. Further changes were made in 1990 with the introduction of summer uniforms with shirts or blouses similar to those worn by police officers.

Local officers' insignia evolved slowly but now they are recognised by the wearing on each shoulder or epaulet of the initials in different colours denoting the position they hold. For example, Corps Secretary: 'C.S.' (yellow), Corps Treasurer: 'C.T.' (blue), Corps Sergeant Major: 'C.S.M.' (red) - but at one time this local officer wore on the upper part of his sleeve four black stripes on a red background with 'C.S.M.' across the stripes.

Bandmasters wear white twisted epaulets, songster leaders wear blue twisted, young people's band leaders wear red twisted and young people's singing company leaders wear red and blue twisted epaulets.

All bandsmen and songsters, most local officers and some soldiers have the name of their corps embroidered on their epaulets, or occasionally at the top of the sleeves.

For many years, to hold their music during open-air meetings and while on the march, bandsman carried a pouch held by a broad white canvas strap worn over the left shoulder.

It should also be added that all Salvationists buy their own uniforms.

Whereas at one time it was generally the custom for men to wear black ties and women black dresses during periods of mourning, Salvationists used to wear on their uniforms a white armband with a red cross on it or a black patch with a red cross sewn on the sleeve. The latter can still be purchased today but are seldom worn.

In looking at family photographs one can generally recognise if an ancestor was a Salvationist by the lady's bonnet or the distinctive 'S', or in some non-English speaking countries the appropriate letter, on the collar. Advice may be needed to establish an approximate date of the photograph and whether the person was an officer or not.

MUSIC

From the early days music and song have played an important part in Salvation Army worship. At first well-known hymns and revival songs were sung and then Salvationists started writing religious words to popular tunes, including those of the nineteenth century music halls. Later, original tunes were composed.

And so today *The song book of The Salvation Army* contains over 1000 hymns, songs and choruses written not only by the great hymn writers like Charles and John Wesley, Isaac Watts and Philip Bliss, but also by Salvationists and contemporary writers.

Singing brigades, later to be known as songster brigades, were formed and in 1886 the first copy of *The Musical Salvationist*, with words and music composed or arranged by Salvationists for these groups was published. Sometimes, particularly in the early twentieth century, solos, duets, quartets, etc. for brass, woodwind,

Swindon II (Old Town) Band - 1886 with the author's grandfather, Captain John Lyons at front with cornet

string and pianoforte and concertina players were also included. It was originally issued monthly and then quarterly. At the end of 1993 it ceased publication and was replaced with separate journals for mixed voices, male voices, female voices and children's voices respectively.

Various musical instruments have from time to time been used in Army meetings, one of the most popular being the concertina which was ideal for accompanying singing, especially in open-air meetings. There were also concertina bands and orchestras. One can only guess what the standard was like in some of these early ones by an advertisement which appeared in *The War Cry* on the 2 March 1882:

> Wanted - FORTY SAVED FIDDLERS or any soldiers who play stringed instruments such as harps, violincellos, guitars, banjoes, etc; to bring their instruments and play at the HOLINESS MEETING held every FRIDAY EVENING at THE OLD HEADQUARTERS, 272 Whitechapel Road, London. The meeting commences punctually at a quarter to eight o'clock led by Mrs Bramwell Booth.

Shortly before its name was changed members of the Christian Mission started to hold meetings in Salisbury and, as in other places already mentioned, its members were attacked by mobs as they preached in the market place. A Methodist builder, Charles Fry, and his three sons, sympathising with them, went to their rescue and linked up with the movement. They all played brass instruments and soon this quartet was standing in the market place, accompanying the singing. From that beginning brass bands became an established part of the Army and today there are over 60,000 bandsmen and women throughout the world.

For many years the Army manufactured its own brass band instruments, starting with two men in a small room in the Trade Headquarters in Southwark Road in London. Eventually a modern factory was established at St Albans, producing first-class instruments. On three occasions the products won gold medals in international exhibitions. In 1972 production ceased and the factory was closed. Some of the staff moved to the works of the well-known instrument manufacturer, Boosey and Hawkes, at Edgware in North West London.

As with songs, music for bands composed or arranged by Salvationists is published at regular intervals in the United Kingdom and throughout the world. In connection with this a Music Editorial Department was set up in 1883 under the supervision of William's son Herbert, who was assisted by Fred Fry and Richard Slater, a converted infidel, who had at one time played the violin under Sir Arthur Sullivan.

Moving with the times, pop groups began to spring up in the 1960s. One of the first and certainly the most successful was 'The Joystrings' which actually got into the charts with its song 'It's an Open Secret'. This decade also saw the introduction of musicals written with good songs, some humour and, most important, an expression of the Christian life and faith.

Many photographs of bands were taken, sometimes with the name of the band and date printed on the bottom. In some the name can distinctly be seen on the flag or, if one looks carefully, painted on the drum. Some, but not so many, photographs were taken of songster brigades with a flag having the name of the brigade on it pinned on the portable organ which was the usual means of accompaniment up to about the late 1950s or early 1960s when it was gradually replaced by a pianoforte.

AWARDS AND COMMENDATIONS

Different orders have been established to recognise the outstanding service which some men and women have given to the Army. For uniformed Salvationists the insignia is worn on the left breast. The orders include:

The Order of the Founder

This was introduced in 1917 by General Bramwell Booth on the fifth anniversary of the death of William Booth, its purpose being to acknowledge such service of any officer or soldier which it was considered would have specially commended itself to William Booth. The first person to be so honoured, in 1920, was Private Herbert J Bourn of the Haggerston Corps whose witness while on active service in France gained for him the title of unofficial chaplain to his battalion. Nearly 200 officers and soldiers have been admitted to the Order since its inception.

The Order of Distinguished Auxiliary Service

This was introduced in 1941 by General George Lyndon Carpenter at the suggestion of a non-Salvationist, Mr Walter Hoving, Chairman of the Board of Directors of Tiffany's in New York, who was the Army's representative during the formation of the United Services Organisation for Defence. It is awarded to mark the Army's appreciation of distinguished service rendered by non-Salvationists who have helped, particularly in a professional capacity, to further the work in a variety of ways. Between 250 and 300 people have been admitted to this Order, the majority of them from overseas.

One such person was Dr D E Menten of The Netherlands who, during the years of occupation in the Second World War, showed his longstanding regard for the Army by gaining for it recognition as a spiritual body, thus enabling Salvationists to continue their work and await with confidence the day of liberation.

Certificate in Recognition of Exceptional Service

This was introduced in 1980 by General Arnold Brown and is awarded to officers, soldiers and friends whose work in or for the Army, although not considered for recommendations to the Order of the Founder or the Order of Distinguished Auxiliary Service, has been of such outstanding value that it should be place on permanent record.

The Order of the Silver Star

This was originally instituted in the USA in 1930 by the then Commander Evangeline Booth. After she became the General she extended it, in 1936, to the rest of the world. It is given to every mother, whether a Salvationist or not, whose son or daughter is serving as an officer as a recognition of the life and example of the mother to her children.

Long Service Badges

Bandsmen, songsters and other local officers who have held office for an aggregate of twenty years are presented with a distinctive badge, with an extra bar for each additional five years service. A different badge is awarded after fifty years service.

Officers are awarded a badge after twenty-five years continuous service and a star to the badge after thirty-five years continuous service.

Retirement Certificates

Officers, local officers, bandsmen and songsters are presented with a certificate when they retire from active service.

CEREMONIES

All Salvation Army ceremonies are of a simple nature and are carried out under the Army flag. After the ceremony the names of the persons concerned are recorded in the appropriate register. Non-Salvationists may be dedicated, married or buried by Salvation Army officers. The main ceremonies are:

Swearing in of Soldiers

This is the public installation ceremony of all Salvationists who have been accepted to become soldiers. During the ceremony the person to be sworn in declares that he will regulate his life according to the Articles of War which he then signs.

Commissioning of Officers

At this ceremony all cadets publicly swear to love and serve God, to make the salvation of souls the first purpose in their life, to maintain the doctrines of The Salvation Army and to prove themselves worthy officers. They then read aloud the doctrines.

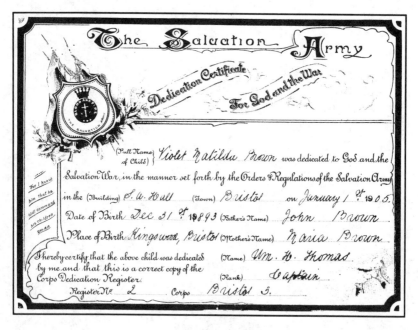

Dedication Certificate of Violet Matilda Brown, Kingswood - 1905

After the ceremony each cadet is called forward and told the place and position to which he or she is being appointed.

Dedication of Children

In place of the christening or baptismal service of most churches the Army has adopted a dedication service, without the use of water. At the service one or both parents thank God for entrusting the life of the child into their hands and promise, so far as they are able, to keep him from everything which is likely to harm him in body, mind and soul, teach him the truths of the Gospels and encourage him to accept the Christian faith. This ceremony is, no doubt, based on the Old Testament story of Hannah dedicating the baby Samuel with her promise that as long as he lived he would belong to the Lord.

Thanksgiving

A simpler form of service than the dedication. In it the parents thank God for the gift of the child and promise, so far as they are able, to keep him from everything likely to harm him in body, mind and soul.

Weddings

On the 12 April 1882 William Booth conducted the wedding of his son, Bramwell, to Florence Soper, and the Salvation Army's Articles of Marriage were drafted for this purpose. With few changes these are in use today. The actual wording of the ceremony is almost identical with those of other churches, and for legal purposes, marriages have to be conducted in the presence of a registrar or authorised person.

For many years it was customary for almost all Salvationists to be married in uniform, the bride wearing a white sash or a spray of flowers. This practice still continues with officers, but since the 1950s, many soldiers wear traditional wedding clothes.

Funerals

The death of a Salvationist is referred to as 'Promotion to Glory'. Again, both the funeral and committal services are very similar to that of other churches.

REGISTERS

A very early issue of *Orders and Regulations for Field Officers* stated that no register was ever to be destroyed and no leaf torn out. As few registers have survived this order appears to have been ignored or, more likely, disappeared into oblivion. For information on those that might still be available see the section on Archives and Memorabilia. Some of these would be regarded as strictly confidential and others, such as Census Board Minute Book, the Cartridge Book, the Commanding Officer's Visiting Book and the Statistics Book, of little interest to the family historian. Those of interest would include:

The Soldier's Roll

The headings in this register include the soldier's roll book number, name, address, where from, married or single, name of officer who enrolled soldier, date of enrolment, if name removed name of officer so doing, reason and date. Obviously, this latter information would be strictly confidential and would not be released to the public.

Dedication, Marriage and Promotion to Glory Register

The headings in the Dedication section include the full name of the child, date of birth, date dedicated, hall where ceremony took place, name of officer who conducted ceremony, signature of parents, signature of witnesses and date

No.	FULL NAME OF CHILD	Date of Birth	PLACE OF BIRTH (Full Address)	Date when Dedicated
1	Fred William Robinson	31-8-1905	Nutfield near Crowboro	16.6.07
2	Robert Edwin Robinson	1.10-1905	" "	16.6.07
3	Harry Noel Robinson	25.12-1906	" "	16.6.07
4.	Ethel Gertrude Bassett	28.8.1907	Spring Cottage Crowborough	Mar. 3.07
	Charles Frank Lee		Spring Cottage Crowborough	
5	Lily Hope.	22:2:1908	6 Queens Road Crowboro	March 29:08
6	Beatrice Rickson	Oct 10. 1898	South View Cottage	June 20th 08
7	William Rickson	Jan 9 1900.	" "	June 20th 08
8	Elsie Hilda Lee	Oct 6th 1908	Haughton Ghyll.	Nov 1st 1908
9	Elizabeth Lilian Packham	September 24th 1909	Whittle, Crowborough	October 24th 1909
10	Stanley Albert Barrett	Oct 19th 1910	Hurtis Hill Crowborough	Dec 18th 1910

Dedication Rigister

32

transferred to Cradle Roll. The names of babies who have been presented at the Thanksgiving Service are also entered in this register.

The headings in the Marriage section include names, dates of birth and full address of the place of birth of both the bride and groom, years of service in the Salvation Army, date of marriage, hall where ceremony took place and the signatures of officer conducting the ceremony, contracting parties and witnesses.

The headings in the Promotion to Glory section include the name of the deceased, date of birth, place of residence, how long a Salvationist, office held, date of death, where interred, number of grave, name of officer who conducted the ceremony, and the date of the funeral.

Transfer Note

When a Salvationist transfers to another corps a Transfer Note is completed in quadruplicate, one copy being handed to the person transferring, one sent to the commanding officer of the new corps, one sent to the divisional ommander of the division he is leaving and one retained in the Transfer Book. When the person has been received at the new corps the copy of the Transfer Note is returned to the former corps.

Information includes the name of the person transferring, how long he has been at the corps, any position held and his new address.

REGISTER

Hall in which Dedicated (Full Address)	Officer who Conducted Dedication (Give Rank and Position)	Names of Parents	Names of Witnesses
Oddfellows Hall Crowborough	Major Arthur Wood	Fredk Wm & Cecilia Robinson	Charles Barton
" "	Ensign G. Casler Benjamin Lynde	Arthur & Ellen Massey	Charles Barton
Oddfellow Hall Crow.	Geo H Hunt Captain	Albert and Alice Hope	May. J. Henshaw J.Sec.
S.A. Hall Whitehill	Geo H Hunt Captain	William & Eliza Rickson	Charles Barton
S.A Hall Whitehill	Geo H Hunt Captain	William & Eliza Rickson	Charles Barton
S.A. Hall Whitehill Rd	Geo H Hunt Captain	Ernest & Esther Lee	Charles Barton
S.A. Hall. Whitehill Rd.	Envoy Surr. (Tonbridge)	Elizabeth & Joseph Packham	Agnes Cottrill. Captain
S.A Hall Whitehill	Adjt Chas Barker	{ Ellen Bassett } { Arthur Bassett }	Bro R. Brown

Crowborough Corps

33

TRACING MISSING PERSONS

In 1885 Mrs Bramwell Booth's Enquiry Bureau, as it was then known, was established to meet the problems of young people missing from home. Many made their way to London seeking work and some, enticed into a life of vice, were too ashamed to write home, so their parents had no knowledge of their whereabouts.

One of the earliest advertisements, headed 'Missing', appeared in *The War Cry* of the 10 October of that year. It concerned a wife, Sarah Barrow, who had disappeared from her home in Widnes in Lancashire. It described her appearance and said that any information about her would be thankfully received by her husband, Thomas Barrow of 13 Elliot Street, Widnes. Such advertisements, occasionally with photographs, continued at intervals and by August 1886 they occupied more than a column.

Even before that, in February 1882, a request was made for any Captain or soldier to look out for a fifteen-year-old boy, Harry Stott, who had run away from home because of the cruelty of his father to his wife and seven children. The father had come under the influence of the Army and been brought to repentance for his behaviour. Harry was described as follows: 'rather tall for his age, brown hair, full grey eyes, cut at corner of left eye, pigeon breasted, right knee bent inwards a little and wearing a black Scotch cap, black coat and waistcoat, light grey cloth trousers and lace up boots'.

A typical announcement in *The War Cry* of the 7 October 1893 stated:

'This Department will SEARCH in any part of the world for missing or runaway relatives or friends; will seek to BRING TO JUSTICE men who have ruined or wronged girls or women; will ENQUIRE into the respectability of people, houses or situations, and generally advise and help, as far as possible, those in difficulty.

Beyond the above it is prepared to undertake detective cases and investigations of certain descriptions for those in a position to pay, at moderate rates.'

Since then thousands of missing persons have been traced through the Army's worldwide network. Husbands who had walked out on their wives and families, people who had emigrated many years earlier and lost touch with their relatives and, brothers and sisters separated from each other as infants have been brought together again. The *Guinness book of records* has recorded that in 1988 a brother and sister, William Pring and Elsie May Ashford, were reunited after being apart for 81 years, having been separated when their mother died in 1907.

The Family Tracing Service is at 105 Judd Street, King's Cross, London WC1H 9TS, telephone number 0171 383 2772. It has a strict policy of absolute confidentiality. All clients must be over seventeen years of age and no searching is made for young people under this age, for those who are just friends or for parents or children separated by adoption or illegitimacy. Officers also occasionally act as counsellors to the people they contact. No case will be followed up if to do so would cause embarrassment to any person involved and no link will be made between any parties should one of them so request.

About 5000 enquiries are received every year and of these contact is made with 75%-80% of those sought. The amount of research is considerable and the time involved can vary from a number of days to several years, although any search taking more than two years would be exceptional. The service is heavily subsidised and, therefore, a small fee is charged on receiving the initial application.

Every weekday at least one member of the staff can been seen at the Family Records Centre searching the indexes to births, marriages and deaths. Other sources used are the police, the Department of Social Security and Dr Barnardo's Homes, an organisation which has very comprehensive records of children who have been in their care.

Where the people being sought are living overseas the information about them is forwarded to Salvation Army personnel in the country concerned. There are actually some Missing Persons Bureaux in certain overseas countries:

Australia	PO Box 486, 308 Edward Street, Brisbane 4000
	PO Box A.435, 140 Elizabeth Street, Sydney
	211 Rundle Street, Adelaide, 5000
	49 Mitchell Street, Darwin 0800
	250 Liverpool Street, Hobart 7000
	333 William Street, Perth 6000
	39 Park Street, Melbourne 3205
Denmark	Frelsens Haer, Frederiksberg Alle 7, 4 sal, 1621, Copenhagen V
France	Armée du Salut, 60 Rue des Frères Flavien, 750020, Paris
Germany	Die Heilsarmee, Sonnensir 10, 6347 Angelburg-Frechenhausen
New Zealand	PO Box 8566, 2 Chambers Street, Havelock N
Norway	Frelsesarmeen, Bernhard Getz' gate 2, 0165 Oslo
Sweden	Frälsningsarmén, Ostermalmsgatan 71, Box 5090, 10242 Stockholm

It must be emphasised that the service is only concerned with tracing living close relatives. It has not the resources to carry out family history research.

THE BOOTH FAMILY

The places where the Booth family lived, the names which William Booth gave to his family, and those they themselves adopted could confuse many a family historian. Some of them were only remotely family names whilst others had no connection whatsoever with the family. His children, all of whom became officers, were:

William Bramwell (1856-1929) - born at Halifax and called after William Bramwell, a well-known preacher. He died at the family home at Hadley Wood in Hertfordshire.

Ballington, (1857-1940) - born at Halifax and called after one of his mother's uncles. He died in the USA.

Catherine (1858-1955) - born at Gateshead and called after her mother but sometimes known as Kate. She died at Ilsington, Devon.

Emma Moss (1860-1903) - born at Gateshead and called after William's sister, Emma, and his mother, Mary Moss. She was seriously injured in a railway accident in Iowa, USA and died shortly afterwards while travelling on a relief train.

Herbert Howard (1862-1926) - born at Penzance and registered as Herbert Henry. He died in New York.

Marian Billups (1864-1937) - born at Leeds and called after Mr J E Billups, a Cardiff industrialist who supported William Booth in his early mission days. Following an accident Marian developed a serious physical weakness and was the only member of the family who did not take a prominent part in the Army. She died at Sunbury on Thames, Middlesex.

Eveline Cory (1865-1950) - sometimes referred to as Emmeline. Born at Hackney and called after John and Richard Cory who were Baptists and well-known South Wales colliery and ship owners who provided financial help to the movement. In 1914 she changed her name by Deed Poll to Evangeline Cory, and was also known as Eva. She died in New York.

Lucy Milward (1868-1953) - born at Hackney and called after her maternal grandmother's maiden name. She died in Stockholm.

There have also been vague, brief references to a ninth child in the Booth household, one Georgie. In the 1881 Census he is recorded as George H Booth, a son born in Hythe, Kent. The next entry is of Harry Andrews (see Medical Work), adopted. There is no record in the indexes at the Family Records Centre of the birth of a George H Booth, nor is there any evidence of Mrs Booth living in Hythe at the time of his birth. One must presume the Census entry is incorrect and George was probably unofficially adopted by the family. The last that was heard of him was in an unpublished letter stating that he had arrived safely in New York in 1890.

When three of the daughters married, their husbands, who had all become officers, added the name Booth to their own surname. Thus Catherine, who married a man of Irish Quaker background, Arthur Sydney Clibborn, became Mrs Booth-Clibborn (their grandson, Stanley, later became the Bishop of Manchester). Emma married Frederick St George de Lautour Tucker, an Englishman who had served in the Indian Civil Service, and became Mrs Booth-Tucker. Lucy married Emanuel Daniel Hellberg, a Swedish officer, and became Mrs Booth-Hellberg.

Bramwell's first child was a girl and when she was born, at his father's suggestion and to ensure the continuance of the name Booth in the family should she ever marry, she was called Catherine Booth Booth. She never did marry and after her father, whom she loved dearly, died, she also changed her name by Deed Poll to Catherine Bramwell-Booth. When she herself died at the age of 104 in 1987, as is common practice with people who have hyphenated names, her death was registered, not only as Booth, Catherine Bramwell, but also Bramwell-Booth, Catherine. Bramwell had six other children, a total of two boys and five girls. Some of his descendants are officers today.

Many Salvationists have given their sons the name Bramwell, sometimes shortened to Bram, although very occasionally Bram, as in the case of the novelist Bram Stoker, is an abbreviation of Abraham. If one finds this name in his searching he can conclude that it is highly likely the child is of Salvation Army parentage.

Others gave their sons the name Booth, Bramwell Booth or William Booth. Some people with such names have been known to hyphenate the name Booth or Bramwell on to their own surname. The only ones with direct relationship with William Booth are those who married his three daughters and their descendants as aforementioned.

ARCHIVES AND MEMORABILIA

Before looking at Salvation Army records it would be important to gain as much information as possible from civil registers, census returns and wills, etc. It would also be helpful if one can establish whether his ancestor was an officer or a soldier.

A number of records are kept at local corps, including registers of soldiers, bandsmen, songsters, etc. In 1907 the official Corps History Book was introduced and a far sighted writer in *The Field Officer* said 'The Salvation Army is rapidly becoming - as a matter of fact, has already become - a people with a history. The idea is not only to make a record of the happenings in the life of any particular corps but to prevent the loss of what will one day prove practically priceless data.' Every corps secretary is expected to enter information of corps activities in the History Book. It should also be added that much of this information would have very little interest to the family historian and in many cases is regarded as confidential. On the other hand some corps officers may be able to point one in the right direction. Their addresses can be found in the local telephone directory under Salvation Army Corps or Officers' Residences.

In May 1941 the Army's headquarters in London was destroyed by incendiary bombs during the Blitz and a great number of records were lost, but many which were deposited elsewhere survived and the following sources will be of interest:

The Salvation Army International Heritage Centre, 117-121 Judd Street, King's Cross, London WC1H 9NN, telephone number 0171 332 8060.

This Centre is open Monday to Friday from 9.30 a.m. to 3.30 p.m. It has a museum displaying a lot of Salvation Army memorabilia and extensive archives. The following list gives some idea of the varied material available for anyone, not only seeking information about his own family, but also wanting to know more about the organisation with which that family was associated:

Administration - Administrative Review (IHQ), Advisory Boards and Councils, Advisory Council to the General, Appointments and Promotions, Articles of War, Audit Department, Bond of Service and Fellowship, British Commissioner, Census Board, Chiefs of Staff, Commissions and Certificates, Committees, Corps Councils, Councils (Officers), Courts of Reference, Development, Discipline (Handbook of), Doctrine Council, Editorial and Literary Department, Female Ministry, Furloughs (Officers), Generals, Homes of Rest, IHQ, International Literary Council, Maps, Marriage Commission, Missionary, Missionary Hostel, Names of the Organisation, Orders and Regulations, Overseas Departments (Foreign Office), Pensions,

Postcodes, Promotions to Glory, Quarters (Officers), Ranks, Resources Departments, Retired Officers' Fellowship, Retired Officers' Residences, Retirement of Officers, Salary, Service Corps, Statistics, Telegraphic Codes, Translators, Uniforms.

Archives, Exhibitions, Museums - Archives, Audio-Visual Aids, Birthplace Museum, British Museum, Christian Resources Exhibition, Computers, Exhibitions, Microfilming, Milsaps Library, Museums, Wembley Exhibition (1924 and 1925).

Arts - Cartoons, Drama, Literature, Music, Paintings.

Awards, Distinctions - Awards, British Empire Medal, Certificate of Recognition of Exceptional Service, Decorations, Freedom of the City of London, Nobel Prize, OBE, Order of Distinguished Auxiliary Service, Order of the Founder, Order of Long Service, Order of the Silver Star, Others.

Buildings, Places - Abney Park, Buildings, Butlin's Holiday Camp, Hotels, Mildmay, Rosehill Conference Centre, Westminster Central Hall.

Business Operations, Organisations - Building Association, Campfield Press, Fire Insurance Corporation, Housing Association, Reliance Bank, Reliance Benefit Society, Reliance World Travel, Salvation Army Assurance Society, Salvation Army General Insurance Corporation, Trade (SP & S Ltd).

Ceremonies, Meetings - Dedication of Children, Love Feasts, Marriage, Meetings, Sacraments.

Christian Mission - Beginnings, Children's Work, Christian Community, Christian Mission League, Names the Organisation had before changing to The Salvation Army.

Community Service, Projects - Agriculture, Camps, Christmas Dinners, Charity Shops, Community Relations, Community Service, Development, Disasters, Dorcas Slum League, Farthing Breakfasts, Gipsies, Goodwill and Slum Work, Handicapped, Holiday Homes, Hospital Visitation, Hotels, League of Mercy, Recycling, Refugees, Waste Paper.

Doctrine - Baptism, Bible, Doctrine, Doctrine Council, Faith-Healing, Prayer, Sacraments, Stewardship, Tongues.

Education, Training - Camps, Company Orders, Corps Cadets, Correspondence Courses, Directory, Education, Mildmay, Missionary Literature, Training, World University of Humanity.

Emergencies, War - Chaplains, Disasters, Red Shield, Refugees, Relief Work, Salvation Army Refugee and Relief Operation, Strikes, Titanic Disaster, War.

Equipment, Symbols - Computers, Crest, Flag, Holiness Table, Penitent Form, Transport, Uniforms.

Evangelism, Mission, Witness - Campaigns, Camp Meetings, Chaplains, Church Growth, Circle Corps, County Evangelism, Cycle Brigade, Evangelism, Flying Padres, Gipsies, Hi! Neighbour, Hyde Park Meetings, Imprisonment and Persecution, Martyrs, Mission Station, Mobile Evangelism, Open-Air Work, Pub Booming, Salvation Navy, Salvation Siege, Skeleton Army, Transport, Visitation, Ward System, Witnessing.

Events, Meetings - Anniversary, Butlin's Holiday Camp, Carol Services, Ceremonies, Congresses, Harvest Festivals, Hi! Neighbour, Meetings, Mothers' Day, Open-Air Meetings, Tickets, Westminster Central Hall Meetings, Women's World Day of Prayer.

External Relations - Auxiliary League, Bible Society, Blue Ribbon Army, British Council, Church Army, Churches and the SA, Critics, Europe 1992, Friends of the SA, Information Services, Jews and the SA, Logo, Mormonism, Opinions of Prominent People, Petitions, Positional Statements, Posters, Press Releases, Public Attitudes to the SA, Public Relations, Public Statements, Quakers, Red Cross, Reports (Annual), Rotary, Royal Recognition, Secret Societies, Spiritualism, UNICEF, United Nations, World Council of Churches.

Fellowship and Service - Blue Shield Fellowship, Butlin's Holiday Camp, Dorcas Slum League, Goodwill League, Home League, League of Mercy, Over 60s Clubs, Red Shield, Salvation Army Medical Fellowship, Salvation Army Refugee and Relief Operation, Salvation Army Students' Fellowship, Widows (work among), Young Women's League.

Finance, Property - Appeals, Audit Department, Auxiliary League, Balance Sheets, Building Association, Buildings, Cartridges, Christmas Kettles, Community and Charity Shops, Community Chest, Finance (Greater London, 1980), Grace Before Meat, Harvest Festival, Housing Association, Legacies, Property, Property League, Reliance Bank, Self-Denial.

Forms, Records - Articles of War, Commissions and Certificates, Cradle Roll, Record Books.

Legal - Copyright, Legal Matters, Salvation Army Trustee Company.

Media, Press - Audio-Visual Aids, Broadcasting, Cinema Photography, Films and Videos, Information Services, Photographs and Photography, Press Cuttings, Press Releases, Recordings, Tape Fellowship, Television.

Medical - Blind (work among), Clinics and Dispensaries, Dentistry, Hydropathy, Homes of Rest, Leprosy (work among), Nutrition.

Moral and Social Issues - Alcoholics and Alcoholism, Community Relations, Debt, Divorce, Environmental Issues, Gambling, Homosexuality, Juvenile Delinquency, Moral Issues, Nuclear Disarmament, Positional Statements, Prostitution, Smoking, Sunday Observance.

Music - Guitars, Junior Musicians, Music (and sub-divisions), Singing Companies.

Naval and Military - Chaplains, Flying Padres, Mariners' League, Red Shield, Salvation Navy, War.

Personnel - Adherents, Auxiliary Captains, Bond of Service and Fellowship, British Commissioners, Candidates, Chaplains, Chiefs of Staff, Corps Cadets, Envoys, Flying Padres, Generals, Hebrew Salvationists, Local Officers, Martyrs, Missionary, Mother Teresa, Recruits, Service Corps, Translators.

Politics - Petitions, Politics and the SA, Salvationists in Public Office, Socialism, Strikes, Suffragettes.

Printing and Publishing - Army Without Guns, Broken Earthenware, Campfield Press, Company Orders, Copyright, Directory, Discipline (Handbook of), Four Bonnets to Golgotha, History of the SA, Jargon, Literature, Major Barbara, Maps, Miscellaneous Memoirs, Missionary Literature, Pall Mall Gazette, Periodicals (circulation figures), Philately and Letterheads, Salvation Standard, Salvationist Index, Trade, Translators, Year Book.

Social Work - Adoption and Fostering, Alcoholics and Alcoholism, Armstrong Case, Black Sacks, Blind (work among), Drug Addiction and Solvent Abuse, Farthing Breakfasts, Harbour Light, Handicapped, Maiden Tribute Case, Mentally Handicapped, Mother Teresa, Pall Mall Gazette, Rehabilitation, Social Services (sub-divisions), Soho Patrol, Widows (work among).

Trade - Advertisements, Almanacs, Bookmarks, Cartoons, Christmas Cards, Clocks, Handkerchiefs, Literature, Maps, Needle Cases, Philately, Postcards, Serviettes, Tea, Toy Soldiers, Trade, Watches, Whistles.

Youth Work - Band of Love and YP Legion, Brownies, Children's Work in The Christian Mission, Children's Year (1971), Company Meeting, Company Orders, Corps Cadets, Cradle Roll, Cubs, Directory, Guards and Guides, Junior Musicians, Junior Soldiers, Postal Sunday School, SABAC, Scouts, Torchbearers and Youth Clubs, Young Women's League, Youth and Young People.

Also of interest to the family historian are:

A reference library of most books published about the Army, together with pamphlets and theses covering all aspects of Salvation Army interest, such as history, orders and regulations, biographies, music, and social and welfare work.

Letters, documents, photographs, programmes.

Corps history books and also centenary brochures which usually record the history of the corps, the names and dates of all officers stationed there and old photographs of personalities, and musical and other groups.

Personnel records of officers.

With limited resources available the staff at the Centre are gradually indexing, on computer, corps reports and lists of officers' appointments from *The War Cry* (from 1879) and *The Officer* (from 1893). These projects are still in their early stages and, therefore, searching has often to be carried out by referring to unindexed volumes.

Members of the public are allowed to carry out research at the Centre by prior appointment with the Archivist. At the present time no charge is made for this.

A small amount of research is carried out by the staff for the public. After an initial search to ascertain what information is available an hourly charge is made for this service.

United Kingdom (with the Republic of Ireland) - The Salvation Army, Territorial Headquarters, 101 Newington Causeway, London SE1 6BU, telephone number 0171 367 4500.

The records include:

> Personnel records, dating back to about the start of the First World War, of all officers who served the whole of their career in Corps in the United Kingdom from the time they entered the Training College for Officers until their death, transfer to headquarters or other appointments or resignation. For information on those so transferred one should refer to the International Heritage Centre.
>
> Information, on careers cards, includes the name of the corps from which the officer entered the Training College, his date of birth and that of his wife and children, dates of marriage, promotions and general information such as his occupation before becoming an officer, if he played a musical instrument, spoke a foreign language or other qualification. If his parents were also officers, their names are recorded. Added to that there is a chronological list of all appointments of the officer and those of his wife before marriage.

Members of the public are not generally allowed to look at this information but copies of non-confidential records will be sent to known relatives on application to the Field Secretary. No charge is made for this service.

William Booth Memorial Training College, Denmark Hill, London SE5 8BQ, telephone number 0171 733 1191.

The records include:

> A complete assessment file relating to each cadet which is compiled during the period from his initial application until his acceptance as being suitable for training. This is passed on to the College by the Candidates Department when he enters the College.

Alphabetical rolls for men and married cadets of each session from 1905 and of women cadets from 1914 which include name of cadet, corps from which he entered Training College, roll number, date entered Training College, date commissioned and rank given on commissioning or if returned home before completing training.

Sessional rolls for women cadets for each session from 1926 and for men and women cadets from 1973 which include name of cadet and, for married couples, wife's maiden name and names of all children, corps from which they entered Training College, date entered Training College, home division, occupation, nationality, age, date of birth, if plays and possesses a musical instrument, if a typist and if experienced in shorthand, if speaks a foreign language, any foreign service and if been a corps cadet.

There are also photobooks in existence of women cadets for the sessions 1911-16, 1918-26, 1928-34, 1936-39 and for all cadets from 1962 onwards. Besides a photograph of the cadet these include most of the information recorded in the sessional rolls.

Since 1987 a total of four Review and Evaluation documents are prepared by cadets and staff together at regular intervals during the two years training period, the purpose of these being to assess progress and identify areas of concern. These are only accessible to the Personnel Secretary and members of the Training College Review Board.

Since 1964 children of cadets may reside at the Training College with their parents.

Members of the public are not allowed to look at these records but information of a non-confidential nature will be supplied on application to the Registrar. No charge is made for this service.

Social Services - The Salvation Army Social Services Headquarters, 101 Newington Causeway, London SE1 6BU, telephone number 0171 383 4230.

The records include:

Information on adoptions and fostering, but the records are of a rather fragmentary nature. They include:

Requests for children to be adopted or fostered. One such, recorded in 1917 in a hand-written notebook, is a request from the wife of an officer in Southall, Mrs Commandant Lyons who, incidentally, was the author's grandmother. She asks for a home to be found for a baby: 'Mrs A's baby was born six months after her husband died from spotted fever, now 14 months old. Her two little girls are in a home and she pays eight shillings weekly. Baby has been with nurse mother but has to be moved.' A reply was sent the following day suggesting a foster mother.

Copies of forms used since 1902 on which are recorded the name of the child and its mother, name of father if known, whether affiliated, date and place of birth, address of Registrar, who has responsibility of the child (mother, local authority, adoptive parents, etc.).

Copies of legal agreements of adoptions.

Information on children who have lived in Army homes up to the present day.

Records of residents of eventide homes are even more sketchy. If application to enter a home was made through headquarters the department has some interview papers, but for women only, as those for men appear to have been lost when the men's and women's social services were amalgamated in 1978. It is unlikely that any old records exist in the homes themselves.

Members of the public are not allowed to look at records but unrestricted information will be supplied on request.

The William Booth Birthplace Museum, Nottingham

The house where William Booth was born, 12 Notintone Place - so named because the bells of nearby St Stephen's did not peal in tune - has been converted by the Army into a museum surrounded by purpose-built premises including an old people's home, flats for homeless families, day centres for the disabled and the elderly, and the provision of meals-on-wheels. A mobile unit for emergency back-up services for floods, fires and other disasters also operates from this complex.

The museum gives visitors a general outline of William Booth's life and the development of the Salvation Army. The room where he was born has been restored and furnished in the early nineteenth century fashion. Other exhibits include his christening robe and wedding waistcoat, caskets and scrolls presented to him on receiving the Freedom of the Cities of Nottingham and London as well as drawings and photographs of Victorian life and Salvation Army history.

Just across the road from the complex is St Stephen's Church, where, in an earlier church on the same site, William Booth was baptized. The baptismal register in which his father is described as a 'gentleman' is in the keeping of the incumbent.

Arrangements to visit the Museum and further information, including a William Booth Walkabout Plan with an audio commentary of the area where his formative years were spent, may be obtained from the Officer in Charge, Notintone House, Sneinton Road, Nottingham, NG2 4QG, telephone number 0115 9503788.

Hackney Archives Department, 43 De Beauvoir Road, London, N1 5SQ, telephone number 0171 241 2886.

The Department has:

Burial registers, some of which are indexed, for Abney Park Cemetery, Stoke Newington from 1840 to 1980 (with gaps 1855-56, 1903, 1933-34). These record the names and dates of burials, details of the costs and charges of each burial together with the plot location code. Later burials in existing graves are also recorded in these registers. Many officers and soldiers are buried here but the cemetery is a conservation area and with the overgrowth of foliage it is often difficult to locate a particular grave.

Maternity register books from Ivy House and the Mothers' Hospital from 1890 to 1959. These record the name and age of the mother, the father's calling (occupation), the address of the nearest relative, name, date and time of birth of the child, religion, if admitted from a Salvation Army home, the name of that home, and names of nurses present at birth. Some of these records may, however, be subject to the 100 years disclosure rule.

Members of the public are allowed to look at certain records by appointment with the Archivist. For postal enquiries a fee-paying arrangement is made with professional record agencies.

St Bartholomew's Hospital, Archives Department, West Smithfield, London EC1A 7BE, telephone number 0171 601 8152.

The Hospital has:

Maternity register books from the Mothers' Hospital from 1913 to 1984 with the same information as those at Hackney Archives.

Members of the public are not allowed to look at these records but information will be supplied to relatives of the persons concerned.

Public Record Office, Ruskin Avenue, Kew, Surrey TW9 4DU, telephone number 0181 876 3444.

BT 27 - Board of Trade Passenger Lists: Outwards (1890-1960). These documents record the ship's name, year and month of sailing, port of embarkation and to which port bound. Also the names, ages, occupational and marital status, of all adult, children and infant passengers and whether of English, Scotch, Irish or foreign nationality.

If one does not know the name of the ship considerable searching is necessary. However, the Salvation Army International Heritage Centre has lists and dates of sailing of a number of ships connected with the emigration scheme.

WO 329 - British War Medal and Allied Victory Medal, Miscellaneous. These documents record the names of members of organisations who served in a civilian capacity with the armed forces during the First World War and for which service they were awarded the above medals. There are separate documents for each organisation and those for Salvationists, mainly officers, include the Salvation Army rank, sometimes the area in which the person served, and any other decorations awarded. Names of men and women are recorded separately.

Overseas Archives Departments

Australia - The Army was officially established in Australia in 1881 and the country is divided into two territories, the Southern Territory and the Eastern Territory.

The Salvation Army Heritage Centre, Southern Territory, 69 Bourke Street, Melbourne, Victoria 3000, telephone number (03) 650 4851.

The Centre has most of the records for both territories and also for the Papua New Guinea Command which until 1994 was part of the Eastern Territory. These include:

> Personnel records of officers, corps and institutional records and personal documents. It also has a collection of publications on immigration but people making enquiries about this subject are referred to the shipping companies which hold the migration records.

Members of the public are allowed to visit the Centre, by appointment, but research is carried out by members of the staff for which no charge is made. There is a charge for postal requests for information about families and also for photocopying documents.

The Salvation Army Heritage Preservation, Eastern Territory, PO Box 63, 120 Kingsland Road, Bexley North, NSW 2207, telephone number (02) 502 0424.

The Centre has some information on officers who have spent most or all of their service in the territory and the Papua New Guinea Command with more information on those of senior rank.

It is open between 10.00 a.m. and 3.00 p.m. and members of the public are allowed to visit it by appointment with the Director. There is a nominal charge for special research, photocopying, laser copying and postage.

Canada - The Army was officially established in Canada in 1884.

The Salvation Army, George Scott Railton Heritage Centre, 2130 Bayview Avenue, Toronto M4N 3K6, Ontario, telephone number 481-4441/2.

The Centre is both a museum and an archive. The museum gives a pictorial outline of Salvation Army history from the beginning in nineteenth century England to the development of the work in Canada up to the present day with the use of artefacts, photographs and special techniques.

A reference library includes various translations of the Bible, religious literature and books on Salvation Army history, social and welfare work, biographies, orders and regulations and musical publications.

The archives include:

Photographs of people, places and events.

A cassette library containing interviews with officers, lay people and speeches of prominent personalities.

Early candidates' rolls, officers' rolls prior to 1914, corps rolls, dispositions of forces, with some gaps, from 1889 to 1994, ledgers, journals, brochures, reports, programmes, slides, films, tapes, etc.

Information on immigration, much of which is fragmentary and not sorted chronologically or alphabetically;

Immigration records on microfilm, including letters from 1885 and also from 1904 to 1909.

Index cards from sailing companies from 1908 to 1958, with gaps.

Bound volumes of sailing sheets from 1915.

Various books and papers.

Sailing sheets.

History sheets of women going to Canada as domestics from 1913 to 1931, giving name, age, home town, date of arrival, name of ship and progress up to four years after arrival.

The Centre is open from Monday to Friday and members of the public are allowed to carry out research by appointment with the Archivist. No charge is made for this. Members of the staff will carry out research for which a charge is made. A charge is also made for photocopying and postage. Group tours of the museum, including those from schools, can be made by prior booking.

Private papers, which are governed by terms of access placed upon them by the donor, and access to certain restricted departmental material is only granted with the permission of the Chief Secretary and the departmental head.

For an annual subscription one may also join the Salvation Army Historical Society which holds meetings and produces a news sheet. Information about this can be obtained from the Heritage Centre.

New Zealand - The Army was officially established in New Zealand in 1883.

The Salvation Army, Territorial Archivist, PO Box 6015, Te Aro, Wellington 6001, New Zealand 1, telephone number 0-4 384 5649.

The Department has the following records:

Personnel records of men and women who applied to become officers or served as such from 1888 to the present day. Also, more detailed information of prominent officers. Access is generally restricted until 70 years after the last entry or 30 years after the death of the person. However, the Archivist does have discretion to release information of a non-controversial nature. Often photographs of these officers are available.

Information which still exists about soldiers will normally be held at the corps at which they were members. If the corps has been closed then records, where they have survived, may have been transferred to the Archives Department.

There are only sparse records of Salvation Army-sponsored child emigrants to New Zealand but there are registers containing names, next of kin and other details of all children admitted to Salvation Army children's homes in New Zealand. Again, access restrictions apply to these files but discretionary release of information is permitted.

Records of residents in rescue and maternity homes from 1887, including birth/adoption records.

Records, often including plans and photographs, of most buildings that have been owned by the Army.

Registers recording most weddings solemnised between 1888 and 1912. Also some up to 1970.

Financial statements, etc. from 1900 and statistical records of field and social work from 1912.

A complete, but unindexed, set of the New Zealand *War Cry* from 1883, many periodicals, pamphlets and books and a large photographic collection.

Members of the public are allowed to carry out research of unrestricted records by appointment with the Archivist. The Archivist and staff are all employed part-time but will answer reasonable requests for information received by post, telephone or fax. No charge is made but donations are gratefully received.

The Salvation Army, Bethany Centre, 35 Dryden Street, Grey Lynn, Auckland 2.

Has records which are rather fragmentary and with some gaps, of all rescue/ maternity homes not held by the Archivist, some dating back to 1887. These include residents' records, hospital and medical records, girls' files, adoptive parents' files and labour records.

Southern Africa - The Army was officially established in Southern Africa in 1883.

The Salvation Army, Territorial Headquarters, 119-121 Rissik Street, Wander-er's View, Johannesburg, 2001, telephone number 403-3614.

It is understood that archives are being collected but no information is available.

USA - The Army was officially established in the USA in 1880 and is divided into four territories, the Central Territory with headquarters in Chicago, the Eastern Territory with headquarters in New York, the Southern Territory with headquarters in Atlanta and the Western Territory with headquarters near Los Angeles.

National Headquarters, The Salvation Army Archives and Research Centre, PO Box 269, 615 Slaters Lane, Alexandria, Virginia 22313, telephone number (703) 684-5500.

The Centre has the following records:

> Personnel records of almost all officers who served in the United States. These are often career sheets and include birth, marriage and death dates and a list of appointments.

> There are also some retirement programmes, funeral programmes and photographs. For more recent and prominent officers there are also articles from the United States *War Cry*, diaries, correspondence and oral histories.

> There are no immigration records.

Members of the public are allowed to carry out research at the Centre by prior appointment with the Archivist. As some records are restricted to staff only it is advisable to check on the availability.

Research is carried out by members of the staff for the public for which no charge is made but a charge is made for photocopying documents and copying photographs.

Western Territorial Museum, 30840 Hawthorne Boulevard, Rancho Palos Verdes, California 90274, telephone number (310) 541-4271.

The territory covers the States of California, Arizona, New Mexico, Nevada, Utah, Colorado, Oregon, Idaho, Washington, Montana, Hawaii and Alaska.

The Museum is not regarded as an archive but has records relating to the territory such as career records of some officers, news cuttings, photographs, etc., some of which have been catalogued on computer records.

Only one member of territorial staff works in the Museum on a part-time basis and carries out searching for the public for which no charge is made except when a large number of photocopies are supplied. The public are not allowed to carry out searches.

PUBLICATIONS

When it was decided to publish the weekly *War Cry* a building in Fieldgate Street, Whitechapel was turned into a printing works. After moving premises two or three times, a modern works was established at St Albans, carrying out a high standard of work from books to leaflets. It was closed in 1992 and today all printing is done by contract. The Army still has printing works in other parts of the world.

A problem the searcher will come across is that, especially in periodicals and particularly in the early days, people were sometimes just referred to as Major Mackenzie, Mrs H, or Songster Leader Mills, etc.,with no initials, let alone their first name. Worse still, one may even find the only identification being 'Auxiliary 784'. At times those on missionary service, particularly in the Indian sub-continent, not only lived as natives, but even adopted native names: John Lyons became known as Dev Kumar (A Prince of the Lord), Staff Captain Paynter as Jai Bhai (Victory Brother), Henry Bullard as Jai Singh, Catherine Bannister as Yuddha Bai (Warrior Sister), Henry Burfoot as Dayasagar (Ocean of Mercy) and Commissioner Frederick Booth-Tucker as Fakir Singh (The Lion of India).

Books

Over the years a great number of books with information about the Army, Salvationists and other people connected with the movement have been published. These range in size from mini-biographies of a few pages to large volumes. Those that are still in print may be purchased from the bookshop at Salvationist Publishing and Supplies Ltd., 117-121 Judd Street, King's Cross, London WC1H 9NN, telephone number 0171 387 1656 or the Mail Order Department, Campfield, St Albans, Herts, AL1 5HY, telephone number 01727 852371.

A very comprehensive and informative book, *A bibliography of Salvation Army literature in English (1865-1987)* has been produced by R G Moyles of the Department of English at the University of Alberta, Edmonton, Canada. In his introduction he says: '... the chief weapon in the Army's war against evil was an arsenal of written documents, pamphlets, magazines, tracts, song books, doctrinal guides, instruction manuals.' Over 2000 books and periodicals are mentioned and the range of subjects can be illustrated by the headings of each section:

History, Description and Public Reaction
Social Service

Promoting the Salvation War
Music and Musical Groups
Salvationist Biography
Autobiographies and Memories
Creative Prose and Poetry
Plays, Poems, Stories by Salvationists
Portraits, Photographs and Cartoons

One can only mention a sample of these publications, some of which have been referred to in compiling this book, but those with the most references to people, many of which have been indexed, are:

General Interest

The history of The Salvation Army.

Volume one - 1865-1878 by Robert Sandall (1947).

Volume two - 1878-1886 by Robert Sandall (1950).

Volume three - Social Reform and Welfare Work by Robert Sandall (1955). *

Volume four - 1886-1904 by Arch R Wiggins (1964). *

Volume five - 1904-1914 by Arch R Wiggins (1968). *

Volume six - 1914-1946 by Frederick Coutts (1973) (also published under the title *The better fight*). *

Volume seven - 1946-1977 by Frederick Coutts (1986).

A hundred years war by Bernard Watson - the history of the Army from 1865-1965 (1965). *

No discharge in this war by Frederick Coutts - the history of the Army from 1865-1974 (1974).

Booth's boots by Jenty Fairbank - social service beginnings in The Salvation Army (1983).

William Booth, founder of The Salvation Army (two volumes) by Harold Begbie (1920).

God's soldier - General William Booth (two volumes) by St John Irvine (1934).

The life of Catherine Booth, the mother of The Salvation Army (three volumes) by Frederick Booth-Tucker (1892-1893).

Bramwell Booth by Catherine Bramwell-Booth (1933).

Salvation dynasty by Brian Lunn - a book mainly about the Booth family (1936).

Some notable officers of the Salvation Army by Minnie Lindsay Carpenter - biographies of twelve officers (1925).

My best men are women by Flora Larsson - stories of the involvement of some 56 women salvationists in various Army activities (1974).

Fighting in many lands, memories of veteran salvationists (1949).

It began with Andrews by Miriam Richards - stories of many officers and other salvationists who served as doctors and nurses in the United Kingdom and countries throughout the world (1971).

Campaigning in captivity by Arch R Wiggins - the experiences of salvationists in Allied, German and Japanese prisoner of war camps during the Second World War (1947).

Overseas Interest

It must be remembered that many pioneer officers in countries throughout the world originated from the United Kingdom and, therefore, one may find the names of ancestors in some of the following history books:

Africa

Banners in Africa by Arthur E Copping (1933).

Our war in South Africa by G S Railton (1901).

The year of jubilee (1883-1933) by W J Barnard.

Alaska

Salvation comes to the last frontier by Evan W Dowling (1986).

Australia

Booth's drum (1880-1980) by Barbara Bolton (1980).

Salvation chariot (1880-1951) by Percival Dale (1952).

Salvation Melbourne - a guide to places of Salvation Army history in Australasia (1992).

Canada

The blood and fire in Canada (1882-1976) by R G Moyles (1977).

The Holy war of Sally Ann by Robert Collins (1984).

The Salvation Army in Newfoundland - its history and essence by R G Moyles (1997).

What God hath wrought (1882-1914) by Arnold Brown (1952).

Caribbean

Jewels of the Caribbean by Doreen Hobbs (1986).

Czechoslovakia

Pioneering in Czechoslovakia by Karl Larsson (1945-1947-1951).

Denmark

Frelsens Hoer i Danmark Gennem 50 Aar by Neils Edelbo (1937).

Germany

Revolutionäres Christentum (two volumes) by Max Gruner (1953-1954).

India

By love compelled by Solveig Smith (1981).

Indonesia

90 tahun Bala Keselamatan di Indonesia - 90 years of The Salvation Army in Indonesia (1984).

Japan

Salvationist Samurai - Gunpei Yamamuro and the rise of the Salvation Army in Japan by David Rightmire (1997).

New Zealand

An outline history of The Salvation Army in New Zealand by Cyril R Bradwell (1950).

Dear Mr Booth (1883-1983) by John C Waite (1963).

Fight the good fight by Cyril R Bradwell (1982).

Women of spirit by Barbara Sampson - biographies of 40 New Zealand women salvationists (1993).

Norway

Femti ars korstog for Gud og Norge by H A Tandberg (1937).

Papua New Guinea

Papuan panorama by George R Carpenter (1957).

Puerto Rico

One hand upon another, The Salvation Army in Puerto Rico by Sallie Chesham (1978).

Rhodesia

Delayed harvest by Victor Thompson (unpublished).

Switzerland

The Salvation Army In Switzerland by Josephine Butler (1883).

USA

Born To battle by Sallie Chesham (1965).

Marching to glory (1880-1980) by Edward McKinley (1980).

Soldiers without swords by Herbert A Wisbey, Jr. (1956).

Zambia

Flag across the Zambezi by Beverley McInnes (1997).

Music and Musicians

Salvation Army song writers by Richard Slater - biographical notes of 70 writers of songs (1930).

Companion to the song book of The Salvation Army by Gordon Avery - stories of how songs appearing in the 1953 song book, came to be written with biographical notes of the writers (1961).

Companion to the song book of The Salvation Army by Gordon Taylor - stories of how songs appearing in the 1986 song book, came to be written with biographical notes of the writers (1989). *

Play the music, play by Brindley Boon - the history of Salvation Army bands (1966).

Sing a happy song by Brindley Boon - the history of Salvation Army songster brigades (1978).

ISB by Brindley Boon - the story of the International Staff Band of The Salvation Army (1985). Over 700 names are recorded in the index to this book.

Index to The Musical Salvationist (1886-1993) compiled by Ray Wiggins (1994) - an unpublished index of over 9000 songs and instrumental compositions giving titles and names of songwriters and composers. Further information can be obtained from the author.

Tracing Missing Persons

God's private eye by Bramwell Pratt (1988) - a book about the Army's family tracing service. No names are mentioned but interesting reading for the family historian.

Missing by Richard Williams (1969) - an earlier book about the Army's family tracing service.

Tracing missing persons by Colin D Rogers (1986) - not a Salvation Army publication but a very useful book with information on searching agencies and the sources one can use in tracing missing persons. *

Copies of those books marked * are at the Society of Genealogists.

The Salvation Army Year Book

Except for two or three gaps in the early years this book has been published annually since 1906. In the introduction to the first number its purpose was explained:

'We hope to be enumerating every country, colony and dependency wherever the Army flag is flying, giving up to date figures of the Army's position, the name of the Territorial Commander and the headquarters address and adding some particulars of the countries yet to be opened, a few facts relating to each of the ten British Centres, Divisions and Corps. Mention is made of every city, town and village in which the Army has a corps.

Facts and figures of interest to officers, soldiers and friends alike will be found in these sections, together with the name of every paper published in all parts of the world, while the Who's Who will be found to contain the names of most of the prominent officers.

Army titles and their meanings will serve as an education to not a few and with a compendium of Army names, institutions and terms the reader is given a brief but concise encyclopedia which should prove of value.

To the officer who is in search of outside statistical information bearing upon drink, crime, pauperism and the like, a section dealing with these various subjects will be helpful.'

The contents of this first number included:

Advertisements
Army Titles and Their Meaning
Assurance
Books and Writers
British Centres, Divisions and Corps
British Provinces
Calendar
Compendium of Army Names, Institutions and Terms
Countries, Colonies and Dependencies
Emigration and Colonisation
Gardeners' Guide
Literature

Outside Facts and Figures
Officers Promoted to Glory during 1905
SA Land Colonies
Social Training
The Great Continents
Useful to Know
Who's Who
World-wide Army

Comparing this with year books of recent times one finds very little difference. Of particular interest are:

A chronological list of Salvation Army history.

Very brief biographies of the Army's founders and all successive Generals.

Names of all active middle ranking officers and retired senior officers, including the date when, and the name of the corps from which, they entered the Training College for Officers, their dates of birth, who they married, similar information about their spouse and their present and previous appointments.

Since 1957 the names of all officers who retired during the previous year and, where appropriate, their wife's maiden name, the last appointment of the officer and the date of retirement.

Names of all officers who died during the previous year and, in the case of married women, their maiden name, the corps from which they entered the Training College and the place and date of death.

A brief description of the history of each territory throughout the world and activities of that territory during the previous year. Also addresses of divisions, social services centres and schools, etc. with names and ranks of leaders and departmental heads.

The doctrines of The Salvation Army.

There is a copy of one of the more recent year books at the Society of Genealogists.

Periodicals

In every country where the Army operates periodicals are published, *The War Cry*, which at one time had a circulation in the United Kingdom of over 300,000 being the most well known. In a few countries the name is different to suit the language of that country but the format is similar. The purpose of every periodical is outlined in *Orders and regulations for Salvation Army editors and members of editorial staff.*

No. 302.   101, Queen Victoria St.   LONDON, SATURDAY, JUNE 4, 1887.   PRICE ONE HALFPENNY.

THE CAMBRIDGE LITTLE SOLDIERS' DRUM AND FIFE BAND.

A Salvation Army children's newspaper

Periodicals of particular interest published in the United Kingdom are:

The East London Evangelist (1868-69) - edited by William Booth, it contained articles and reports from missioners and obituaries under the title 'Our friends in Heaven'.

The Christian Mission Magazine (1870-78) - contained articles, reports of stations, plans of services, places of meetings and names and addresses of preachers, exhorters and prayer leaders.

The Salvationist (1879) - a successor to *The Christian Mission Magazine.*

The War Cry (1879) * - published weekly and still in print.

The first edition of 17,000 copies was a four-page paper sold at one halfpenny per copy. In introducing it William Booth wrote: 'to attempt to represent the work in more than 120 places within the pages of a monthly periodical is no longer possible ... We shall have plenty of room for every- body and everything connected with the Service ... We shall try to give the news from every Station ... stories of disgraceful failures as well as magnificent successes, omitting, of course names when advisable ... The paper will be the Official Gazette of the Army.'

This edition not only included reports from stations, but a list of all officers and where they were stationed, and the names of officers awaiting appointments were recorded. It was also reported that four officers, unnamed, had been reduced to the ranks; two for light and frivolous conduct and conversation, one for contracting a matrimonial engagement immediately after appointment without the consent of headquarters, and one for misbehaviour in the presence of the enemy.

As it became established, regular features to be found were reports from corps, centres and overseas territories, photographs, biographies of and appointments and tranfers of officers. Also obituaries of officers and soldiers. In 1986 its format was changed so as to be a religious paper for the non-salvationist - see *Salvationist* below.

The Little Soldier (1881-1887) * - contained stories and news, including obituaries, about Salvationist children.

The Young Soldier (1888) * - a successor to *The Little Soldier*, changing its name in 1990 to *YS* and in 1996 to *Kids Alive!*

In 1932 this paper published a series of photographs, taken up to forty years earlier, of well-known officers and their families with heading 'Who Are These?'. On another page the answer was given. One such stated that: 'The photograph was of the late Staff Captain William and Mrs Hodgson and their children. Brigadier Herbert is on I.H.Q., Staff Captain John W. at the Men's Social Headquarters, Band Secretary Alfred was promoted to glory at sea in 1909 when on his way to England to enter training. The daughters are respectively, Mrs Colonel Barr, Korea, Mrs Brigadier Penfold, U.S.A., and Mrs Major Taylor, Java. A separate adjacent photograph was of Mrs Brigadier Herbert as a little girl.' A good example of how officers served all over the world and the difficulty one might find in trying to locate them.

The Y.P. (1906-1910) - contained articles and photographs of interest to young people between 15 and 21 years of age.

The Warrior (1911-1955) - a successor to *The Y.P.*

Vanguard (1955-1972) - a successor to *The Warrior*. After 1972 it appeared every two weeks as an eight page pull-out supplement in *The War Cry* entitled *Youth Focus*.

The Local Officer (1897-1908) - contained news, photographs and articles, all of which would be of interest to people in lay positions in the Army. The first volume contained articles on The Treasurer and His Work, Notable Bands and an obituary of Bandmaster MacDonald of Londonderry.

The Bandsman, Local Officer and Songster (1907-1937) * - a successor to *The Local Officer*, changing its name to *The Bandsman, Songster and Local Officer* and, finally, *The Bandsman and Songster*.

In introducing the paper William Booth said: 'It will tell of the last tune, the latest wonderful march, the last remarkable superior instrument turned out at St Albans. Here will be set forth photographs, reproductions of first one band or songster brigade and then another.'

Regular features included technical articles, reports of musical festivals, announcements of births, marriages, obituaries, appointments, transfers to other corps, and photographs of musical personalities and groups as well as wedding photographs.

Looking through the bound volume for 1923 one finds, among other things, photographs of bands from Montreal, Berlin, Lagos, Nairobi and Chicago, an article by Corps Sergeant Major Robert Bishop Farrow of the Grimsby 1 Corps about local officers who have served there for many years, another about Corps Treasurer William Morris of Harlesden who, as reported in a number of national newspapers, had recently been made the first driver of 'The Caerphilly Castle' which was the most powerful passenger locomotive in the country.

There was also correspondence from a number of people naming relatives playing in the same bands.

The Musician of The Salvation Army (1938-1986) - a successor to *The Bandsman and Songster*, double the size and with the addition of more material relating to young people's bands and singing companies.

Salvationist (1986) - a periodical incorporating material relating to Salvationists previously published in *The War Cry* and *The Musician of The Salvation Army*.

All the World (1884) - a monthly magazine, still published today, to provide information on the development of the work overseas.

The Deliverer (1889-1923 and 1928-1993) - the organ of the women's social work, originally a monthly record of the rescue work featuring, among other things, requests for information on missing persons. In more recent years a family magazine.

Values (1994-1996) - a successor to *The Deliverer*. A Christian magazine with news, views, letters and advice of particular interest to the family

The Social Gazette (1893-1917) - the organ of the men's social work, initially known as *The Darkest England Gazette*.

The Officer (1893) - a monthly magazine for private circulation among officers. At times its name was changed to *The Field Officer*, then *The Officers' Review* before reverting to its original title.

The first edition contained news items, names and places of officers who had changed appointments, guidance notes on preparing sermons, organisation, raising money and other matters. The December issue of 1893 mentioned a novel form of amplification: 'Staff Captain Fred Cox had written to say that he had been trying an experiment with success. By holding the drum - tightened - level with the chest, and speaking so that the voice falls upon the parchment, it increases the volume of sound, and makes the speaking out of doors very much easier, besides being heard at a greater distance. He has also tried singing with similar results.'

The Life Saving Scout and Guard (1921-1948) - contained stories, articles of a practical matter, reports, photographs etc. relating to Salvation Army Scout, Guard, Chum and Sunbeam troops and members throughout the world.

The Scout and Guard (1948-1955) - in 1948 the Salvation Army Scout movement was affiliated to the Boy Scout movement and the words 'Life Saving' were deleted from the title of the magazine for members.

Assurance (1898-1970) - the house magazine of the Salvation Army Assurance Society. The title was changed from time to time to *Head Office Review* and *The Assurance Magazine*.

Copies of those periodicals marked * are at the British Newspaper Library, Colindale Avenue, Colindale, London NW9 5HE, telephone number 0171 323 7353.

GLOSSARY OF SALVATION ARMY TERMS

Many of these terms are no longer in use.

Adherent - A person who regards the Salvation Army as his or her spiritual home but is not committed as a soldier.

Agent Captain - An officer on probation appointed to take command of a Circle Corps.

Altar Service - A time set aside during a meeting at the appropriate time of the year for Salvationists and friends to make a personal donation to the Self-Denial, Harvest Festival and other special appeals.

Articles of War - The statement of beliefs and promises which every soldier is required to sign before enrolment.

Auxiliary - A friend of the Army who contributed a certain sum annually to its support.

Auxiliary Captain - A mature salvationist, beyond the age limit for full time officer training, who holds a position similar to an officer and may undertake full-time paid corps or social work.

Band League - A group of people who generally contribute a weekly sum to assist the band's finances.

Band of Love - A junior section of the Young People's Legion.

Barracks - The early term for a building where meetings were held.

Blood and Fire - The Army's motto which refers to the blood of Jesus Christ and the fire of the Holy Spirit.

Booming - see Pub Booming.

Bridge Programme - A rehabilitation programme for alcohol and drug dependants, usually operating in Australia and New Zealand.

British Commissioner - The territorial commander of the United Kingdom and the Republic of Ireland.

Cadet - A Salvationist now on a two year course of training for officership. At one time the period was much shorter.

Candidate - A Soldier who has been accepted for officer training.

Cartridge - The Salvationist's regular financial contribution towards corps expenses.

Census Board - Local officers in a corps responsible for adding or removing names from the rolls. (The name was changed to the Pastoral Care Council in 1998.)

Chief of Staff - The officer second-in-command of the Army throughout the world.

Chief Secretary - The officer second-in-command of a territory.

Chums - Originally the Army's equivalent of Cubs.

Circle Corps - A group of at least three societies.

Citadel - A name often used for buildings where meetings are held.

Colours - The tricolour flag symbolising the blood of Jesus Christ (red), the fire of the Holy Spirit (yellow) and purity of God (blue).

Command - A smaller type of territory, directed by an officer commanding.

Company Guard - A person who takes a class in the Sunday school.

Congress - Central gatherings, usually held annually in a territory, region or division.

Corps - The Salvation Army's local church and its members.

Corps Cadet - A young Salvationist who undertakes a weekly course of Bible study, doctrine and public speaking training.

Corps Council - A committee set up to advise the commanding officer on such matters as fund raising, building projects, publicity and welfare work, etc.

Corps Secretary - A local officer responsible to the corps officer for administration matters and, with the Corps Treasurer, for financial matters.

Corps Sergeant Major - A local officer responsible to the corps officer for open-air meetings and who usually looks after the public work in the officer's absence. He will also make any announcements in the meetings.

Corps Treasurer - A local officer responsible to the corps officer for the whole of the finances of the corps, assisted in this responsibility by the Corps Secretary.

Cradle Roll - A record of babies in the corps.

Dedication Service - A ceremony where babies are dedicated (see Ceremonies).

Division - A number of corps, social services and public relations departments grouped together under a divisional commander.

Elevator - A labour factory where men were given employment such as wood chopping and collecting and sorting waste paper.

Envoy - A local officer appointed to conduct meetings and sometimes take charge of a small corps.

Evangeline Residence - The name used in some countries for centres providing a 'home away from home' for young business women and college students.

Ex-Soldiers Sergeant - A person responsible for seeking the restoration of former Salvationists.

Field Battery - A light one-horse van used for outside services, provided with two berths and accommodation for two men.

Fishing - A practice once used whereby Salvationists spoke to members of the congregation in a prayer meeting for the purpose of encouraging them to accept the Christian faith or commit themselves to fuller service. (From Jesus' call to Peter and Andrew: 'Follow me, and I will make you fishers of men.' - Matthew 4:19).

Goodwill Centre - A centre in poorer areas of large cities to render practical aid to needy and under-privileged persons.

Grace Before Meat - A scheme for raising funds for social services by means of sums placed in a box in private homes, offices or shops.

Harbour Light Centre - A centre for the rehabilitation of alcohol and drug dependants, usually operating in Canada and the USA.

Herald - A person who sells Salvation Army periodicals.

Home League - A women's fellowship holding weekly meetings.

Knee Drill - A prayer meeting usually held early on a Sunday morning.

League of Mercy - Salvationists who visit prisons, hospitals and needy homes, bringing the Gospel and rendering practical aid.

Life Saving Guards - Originally the Army's equivalent of Guides.

Local Officer - A person appointed to a position of responsibility in a corps.

Mercy Seat or Penitent Form - A bench, usually situated between the platform and the main area of Army halls, where people can kneel to pray, seek salvation or make special consecration to God's will and service. (From God's instruction to Moses to make a lid for the ark of the covenant - a mercy seat - and saying: 'There I will meet with thee, and I will commune with thee from above the mercy seat.' - Exodus 25:17-22).

Organising Secretary - A person appointed to organise special events like musical programmes and visits from other bands and songster brigades.

Outpost - A locality in which Army work is carried out from time to time and where it is hoped a society or corps will develop.

Pastoral Care Council - Local Officers in a corps who review the rolls of soldiers, recruits, adherents and friends of the corps and discuss their pastoral needs.

Penitent Form - see Mercy Seat.

Prison Gate Home - A temporary reception centre for released prisoners and parolees.

Promotion to Glory - The Army's description of the death of a Salvationist.

Pub Booming - The selling of Army papers in public houses.

Publications Sergeant - A person responsible for selling periodicals.

Quartermaster - A handyman responsible for small maintenance of corps property.

Reconciliation Bureau - A department that attempted to settle family and domestic quarrels.

Red Shield Appeal - A term now used for the Self-Denial Appeal.

Red Shield Centre - A club for Armed Forces personnel.

Recruiting Sergeant - A local officer responsible to the corps officer for training people who are being considered to become soldiers and adherents, in the doctrines and regulations of the Salvation Army. Also to counsel people who seek spiritual guidance at the mercy seat.

Reservist - A retired bandsman or songster.

SABAC - The Salvation Army Boys' Adventure Corps, an outreach programme for boys.

Self-Denial Appeal - An annual effort to raise funds for the Army's worldwide operations.

Slum Post - the former name of a Goodwill Centre.

Society - A small company of soldiers working in a district.

Sunbeams - Originally the Army's equivalent of Brownies.

Territorial Commander - The officer in charge of a territory.

Thanksgiving Service - A ceremony where parents give thanks to God for the gift of a child.

Torchbearer Group - A youth club.

Veteran's Secretary - A person appointed to carry out visitation of the aged and infirm.

Warrant Officer - The early term for a local officer.

Welcome Sergeant - A person who stands at the entrance to the hall to welcome people to the meetings.

Young People's Legion - A children's club.

Young People's Sergeant Major - The superintendent of the Sunday school.

ABBREVIATIONS

AC	Auxiliary Captain
BM	Bandmaster
CCG	Corps Cadet Guardian
CHQ	Command Headquarters
CO	Commanding Officer
CS	Chief Secretary, Corps Secretary
CSM	Corps Sergeant Major
CT	Corps Treasurer
CYO	Command Youth Officer
CYS	Corps Youth Secretary
DBM	Deputy Bandmaster
DC	Divisional Commander
DDWO	Divisional Director of Women's Organisations
DFO	Divisional Finance Officer
DHQ	Divisional Headquarters
DS	Divisional Secretary
DSL	Deputy Songster Leader
DYPS	Divisional Young People's Secretary
DYS	Divisional Youth Secretary
FM	Field Major
FO	Field Officer
GW	Goodwill Centre
HLS	Home League Secretary
HLT	Home League Treasurer
HF	Harvest Festival
ICO	International College for Officers
IHQ	International Headquarters
ISB	International Staff Band
IS	International Secretary
ISS	International Staff Songsters
ITC	International Training College
JS	Junior Soldier
LoMS	League of Mercy Secretary
MSS	Men's Social Services
MSW	Men's Social Work
NHQ	National Headquarters

O&R	Orders and Regulations
OC	Officer Commanding
OSCS	Over-60 Club Secretary
OSCT	Over-60 Club Treasurer
pG	Promoted to Glory
PGB	Prison Gate Brigade
PO	Provincial Officer
PRB	Public Relations Bureau
PRD	Public Relations Department
PRO	Public Relations Officer
(R)	Retired
RS	Red Shield
	Recruiting Sergeant
SAAS	Salvation Army Assurance Society
SABAC	Salvation Army Boys' Adventure Corps
SAFE	Salvation Army Fellowship of Endeavour
SAGIC	Salvation Army General Insurance Corporation
SAMF	Salvation Army Medical Fellowship
SASB	Salvation Army Song Book
SASF	Salvation Army Students' Fellowship
SB	Song Book
SC	Staff Captain
SD	Self-Denial
SocS	Social Services
SL	Songster Leader
SP&S	Salvationist Publishing and Supplies Ltd.
TB	Tune Book
TC	Territorial Commander
TG	Training Garrison
THQ	Territorial Headquarters
TMC	Territorial Music Council
TP	Training Principal
TPWO	Territorial President for Women's Organisations
TSB	Territorial Secretary for Bands and Songster Brigades
TYS	Territorial Youth Secretary
TYCL	Torchbearer Youth Club Leader
WSS	Women's Social Services
WSW	Women's Social Work
YP	Young People
YPBL	Young People's Band Leader
YPSCL	Young People's Singing Company Leader
YPSM	Young People's Sergeant Major
YS	Young Soldier